W9-BGZ-467

Other Books By J. R. Ackerley
Published by Poseidon Press

My Dog Tulip

My father and myself

My Father and Myself

J.R. Ackerley

Poseidon Press

New York · London · Toronto
Sydney · Tokyo

Copyright © 1968 by The Executors of the late J. R. Ackerley
All rights reserved
including the right or reproduction
in whole or in part in any form.
Published by Poseidon Press
A Division of Simon & Schuster, Inc.
Simon & Schuster Building
Rockefeller Center
1230 Avenue of the Americas
New York, NY 10020
POSEIDON PRESS is a registered trademark of Simon & Schuster, Inc.
Published by arrangement with G. P. Putnam's Sons,
a Division of The Putnam Publishing Group
For information address G. P. Putnam's Sons,
200 Madison Avenue, New York, NY 10016

Manufactured in the United States of America

10   9   8   7   6   5   4   3   2   1

Library of Congress Cataloging in Publication Data
Ackerley, J. R. (Joe Randolph), 1896–1967.
   My father and myself.

   Reprint. Originally published: London: Bodley Head, 1968.
   1. Ackerley, J. R. (Joe Randolph), 1896–1967.
2. Homosexuals—Great Britain—Biography.   3. Fathers
and sons—Great Britain.   I. Title.
HQ76.3.G7A24   1988   306.7′662   87-25769

ISBN 0-671-65675-9

To Tulip

ILLUSTRATIONS

My father and myself (*frontispiece*)

FOREWORD

THE apparently haphazard chronology of this memoir may need excuse. The excuse, I fear, is Art. It contains a number of surprises, perhaps I may call them shocks, which, as history, came to me rather bunched up towards the end of the story. Artistically shocks should never be bunched, they need spacing for maximum individual effect. To afford them this I could not tell my story straightforwardly and have therefore disregarded chronology and adopted the method of ploughing to and fro over my father's life and my own, turning up a little more sub-soil each time as the plough turned. Looking at it with as much detachment as I can command, I think I have not seriously confused the narrative.

J. A.

*My
Father
and Myself*

One

I was born in 1896 and my parents were married in 1919. Nearly a quarter of a century may seem rather procrastinatory for making up one's mind, but I expect that the longer such rites are postponed the less indispensable they appear and that, as the years rolled by, my parents gradually forgot the anomaly of their situation. My Aunt Bunny, my mother's younger sister, maintained that they would never have been married at all and I should still be a bastard like my dead brother if she had not intervened for the second time. Her first intervention was in the beginning. There was, of course, a good deal of agitation in her family then; apart from other considerations, irregular relationships were regarded with far greater condemnation in Victorian times than they are today. I can imagine the dismay of my maternal grandmother in particular, since she had had to contend with this very situation in her own life. For she herself was illegitimate. Failing to breed from his wife, her father, whose name was Scott, had turned instead to a Miss Buller, a girl of good parentage to be sure, claiming descent from two admirals, who bore him three daughters and died in giving the last one birth. I remember my grandmother as a very beautiful old lady, but she was said to have looked quite plain beside her sisters in childhood. However, there was to be no opportunity for later comparisons, for as soon as the latter were old enough to comprehend the shame of their existence they resolved to hide it forever from the world and took the veil in the convent at Clifton where all three had been put to school. But my grandmother was made of hardier stuff; she faced life and, in course of time, buried the past by marrying a Mr Aylward, a musician of distinction who had been a Queen's Scholar at the early age of fourteen and was now master and organist at Hawtrey's Preparatory School for Eton, at Slough. Long before my mother's fall from grace, however, he had died, leaving my grandmother so poor that she was reduced to doing needlework for sale and taking in lodgers to support herself and her growing children. What could have been her feelings to hear the skeleton in her family cupboard, known then only to herself, rattle its bones as it moved over to make room for another?

Nevertheless, it seems to have been left to my Aunt Bunny, her younger daughter, to exhibit the deepest sense of outrage at my father's behaviour and to administer the sternest rebuke. This, to anyone who knew my aunt, might be thought strange, for she was the jolliest, cleverest and least conventional member of an unconventional family. She was, in fact, at this time its main financial support by her engagements as a vocalist, a mezzo-soprano of concert platform and operatic standard, though her great promise was soon to collapse and reduce her to light opera and musical comedy, understudying Connie Ediss at the Gaiety Theatre, and provincial touring companies in anything that offered. But her moral position did not lack strength, for she had lately, in 1890, contracted an orthodox union with a gambler named Randolph Payne; moreover she was always a formidable champion of the rights of her own sex. However, she failed, as everyone else failed, to persuade my father to make an honest woman of my mother and punished him by declaring that she would never speak to him again. Nor did she for ten years; but then, since her hostile attitude was seen to be as inconvenient as it was ineffective, she relented, a reconciliation took place and she and my father became firm friends. Besides, the test of time had already made it ironically clear that while my father and mother had attained happiness, fortune and good repute without the blessing of the Church, holy wedlock with Uncle Randolph had brought my aunt nothing but shame and privation.

At the time of her second intervention, in 1919, she was, of course, a middle-aged woman and, if aspects can sit, the moral aspects of the matter had taken a back seat. She was concerned now, more practically, for my mother's financial future and what, in this respect, would happen to her in the event of anything happening to my father; taking advantage, therefore, of a pleasant opportunity when she was dining with him alone, she summoned up her courage, for he was a king, if only a banana king, and an authoritative sort of man, and asked him boldly whether, in fairness to my mother and their two surviving children, he had not better marry her after all. Much to her surprise and relief, he 'very sweetly' accepted her advice. This historic event occurred at Pegwell Bay in the spring of the year, and my aunt, full of her triumph, urged my mother to hold him to his promise without further loss of time, in case he changed his mind, or, since his blood pressure was known to be high, something less disputable happened to him. But my mother, who was liable to inconvenient Eastern superstitions, announced that she had always wished to be married on October the thirteenth, her lucky day, and no other date would do. The ceremony was therefore postponed until then and involved my aunt, who was to be one of the witnesses, in a troublesome railway journey, for she was touring with Cyril Maude in *Lord Richard in the Pantry* and had to come up from Cardiff during the run of the play. The wedding took place quietly at St George's, Hanover Square, in the presence of my aunt and her second husband, an inebriate named Dr Hodgson Chappell Fowler, who were now the only sharers in my parents' guilty secret.

There were, as it happened, far more cogent reasons for this tardy rectification of their relationship than my aunt was aware of at the time. They were not to be known by her, or any member of the family, until after my father's death ten years later, by my mother, who survived him seventeen years, never at all, and the irony of this situation appeared in the last decade of my mother's life when my aunt, widowed for a second time and again left penniless, became a poor pensioner upon her charity, lived with her in some disharmony and was occasionally made to feel the dependence of her position. It sometimes then suited her *amour-propre* to remind my mother of the signal service she had rendered her twenty years ago; but although she was free to recall her intervention as a successful piece of diplomacy, she was unfortunately morally precluded from revealing the facts that had come to her knowledge since and lent to her intervention, in retrospect, so momentous a character. This crippled claim to importance brought her no reward more visible than self-satisfaction; the last thing my mother wished in alcoholic and eccentric old age was to acknowledge any obligation to her sister; after attempting, therefore, to challenge the truth of the story, a manoeuvre my aunt stoutly resisted, she would dismiss it with 'Oh well, he would have married me in his own time anyway', to which my aunt, who was also addicted to the last word, replied, 'Yes, I don't think!'

But the subject, beyond providing one of the several battle-fields between the two old ladies, was not otherwise mentioned, and I might never have known that I was for so many years a social outcast if my mother had not once, in a moment of vexed self-pity, rashly disclosed the fact to my sister who, though pledged to secrecy, promptly passed it on to me. I was, of course, delighted. My mother, whom I had seldom been able to take entirely seriously, now acquired in my eyes heroic proportions; but unhappily it turned out that she was far from taking so romantic a view of herself, for when she learned that I too was in possession of her secret she became very agitated, vehemently denied the whole thing and implored me, unless I wished to make her ill, never to speak of it again. I was thus unable to discuss it with her, which I should greatly have liked to do, until, many years later, she herself brought it out one evening, quite casually and without a trace of embarrassment as one might talk about the weather; but by that time unfortunately she had almost completely lost her memory and could recall of her past no more than that now somewhat mechanical repertoire of anecdotes with which, from constant repetition, I was already over-familiar. She could not therefore satisfy my curiosity about her early life with my father, and such information as I possess is derived from other sources, principally from my Aunt Bunny who outlived her.

Two

THEIR first encounter was in the autumn of 1892. My mother was going over to Paris to stay with some friends and was being seen off at Victoria Station by her mother, Aunt Bunny and Charles Santon the singer. Upon the platform also, sauntering up and down, was a tall, handsome, elegantly tailored young man, of military bearing, with a fine fair moustache and a mourning band round one arm, who regarded my mother with noticeable attention. Certainly she was attractive, pretty, *petite*, and vivacious, and, according to my aunt, by no means unaware of the existence of young men. The handsome gentleman was also bound for the Continent, but first class; my mother, whose family had fallen upon hard times, was travelling third—only, added my aunt drily, because there was no fourth.

This is *her* version of the original encounter which was later to be of such consequence to myself; my mother modestly preferred to ignore Victoria Station. She staged the first moment of mutual awareness a trifle more romantically, in mid-Channel, when she was looking about for a steward to bring her a dry biscuit and some lemon as a preventive of sea-sickness. The sea was calm, and if my mother was failing to attract the attention of a steward, she was not failing, as she 'gradually noticed', to attract that of a handsome, soldierly young man, with a fine fair moustache, who was pacing the deck before her and casting in her

direction glances of unmistakable interest. At length he
was emboldened to approach her, and addressed her in so
chivalrous a manner that it was impossible to take offence,
his actual words, according to my mother, being 'I see you
are in difficulties. If I can be of any assistance, pray command
me.'

Such a gentlemanly speech (which, in years to come, my
mother delighted to recount at dinner parties, in sentimental
and dramatic tones, while my father looked self-consciously
down his nose) was reassuring, he was sent for the biscuit
and lemon and permitted to escort her on to Paris, which
was his own destination. How the difference in their classes
was adjusted my mother could not recollect, but it remained
in her memory that he possessed an exceedingly beautiful
travelling-rug which he solicitously wrapped about her, for
the air in the Channel had been fresh. During the journey
she learnt that his name was Alfred Roger Ackerley, that
he was twenty-nine, a year older than herself, that he was
lately bereaved of his wife, a Swiss girl who had died only a
few months previously after scarcely two years of married
life, and that the object of his journey to Paris was to visit his
in-laws, who lived there. He seemed much affected by his
loss; my mother used to say in later years, 'He came to me a
broken man,' and I think it may have been for him a severe
blow, for he rarely spoke to us about that period of his life
or mentioned his first wife's name, which was Louise
Burckhardt. She was a friend of Sargent's, and a portrait of
her by him, 'The Lady with the Rose', is in the Metropoli-
tan Museum of Art, New York. It seems unlikely therefore
that my father fell in love with my mother so soon after his
bereavement, but he clearly found her attractive—and

indeed, from her photographs at that time and her appearance and character as I remember her, she must have been a charmer. He called upon her at her friend's house several times, leaving cards and flowers, for she was always out, and, without having found her again, sent more flowers to await her at the train by which he learnt she was leaving at the conclusion of her visit.

Their second meeting took place in the early summer of the following year, again upon water, this time the fashionable reaches of the river Thames. My mother was staying at Chertsey with her mother, Aunt Bunny, and Bunny's first ne'er-do-well husband, Randolph Payne, and they were all boating one day through Shepperton, Bunny at the oars, when a voice hailed them from a passing punt. Who should it be but Alfred Roger Ackerley, who was living, it appeared, a comfortable bachelor's life in a house in Addlestone. To describe this second meeting thus, as my mother used to describe it, invested it with the romance of happy coincidence; actually they had been in correspondence in the interval and young Mr Ackerley had already paid luckless calls and left cards upon her in her Chertsey lodgings. My mother had by now quite an accumulation of his cards and was 'overcome by confusion', she said, when he discovered that she had preserved them all.

Calls were exchanged and Bunny was taken one day to tea with him at the Addlestone house, a visit which, according to her, was not an unqualified success, for their host paid her (whom he had nicknamed 'the Boy' because of her prowess with the sculls and the punt pole and her general independence of spirit) rather more attention than my mother liked and recriminations between the two young ladies ensued during their homeward journey. But my mother need not have upset herself. She was not to be neglected. Eighteen months later, in the spring of 1895, she was pregnant and my father was declining to marry her. The reason he gave was indeed substantial; he was receiving a princely allowance of £2000 a year from his in-laws, Mr and Mrs Burckhardt, who regarded him more as a son than a son-in-law, and this allowance, which was to be perpetuated in Mr Burckhardt's will, might well cease with his re-marriage. However, this excuse, though weighty at the time, was scarcely valid for a quarter of a century, the less so since Mr Burckhardt died suddenly and intestate at the end of this very year, so that my father's expectations came to nothing—nor apparently did it satisfy Aunt Bunny. She, indeed, was in a position to take of my father's conduct and character a more objective view than was available to my mother, for she had, with regard to him, inside information, confidentially supplied by my Uncle Randolph, confidentially supplied to him by my father, with whom he had become pally, that at this same period my father was amusing himself with other women elsewhere: there was a certain Mrs Carlisle, who lived vaguely, but appropriately, 'in the North', and he had also informed Randolph that two of the barmaids at the Chertsey Bridge Hotel were 'all right'.

Three

AUNT BUNNY used to say that there was a strong streak of coarseness in my father's nature—and who should be better able than she to recognise it? It was specially evident, she said, in some of his ideas about women. In fact, as I remember him, his social manners towards women were admirable, always courteous, indeed gallant; it is also true that in male company he was liable to refer to pleasing specimens of the female sex who caught his eye in the street as 'plump little partridges'. This predatory, gastronomic approach to women would certainly not have suited my aunt; in spite of her gay spirits and general *camaraderie*, in spite of her ready and robust sense of humour, in spite of her being a 'jolly good sport' and 'the Boy', she was, I believe, fundamentally virtuous, she drew the line, and in her own reminiscences all the unfortunate men, except the two duds she chose to marry, who attempted to overstep it and take liberties towards herself or her particular girl friends, were always described as 'dirty' or 'nasty' old men, who got what they deserved from her fist, her nails, or her foot. She was something of a Mae West in her character, with an extraordinarily infectious chesty laugh, which I used to call her Saloon Bar laugh, a fund of amusing, *risqué* stories and ditties, and a staunch loyalty to all her men and women friends; but I have a suspicion that she, and my mother too for that matter, never found the sexual act agreeable or hygienic.

It is necessary to know about my father that he had been a guardsman. He was born on April 1, 1863, the seventh of a large family of three boys and five girls, in Prospect Cottage, Rainhill, a village near Liverpool. His father, who described himself as a share-broker, came a financial cropper in 1875 and had to remove his family to a smaller cottage nearby and send the children out to work. The girls took jobs as teachers, the boys were put to trades, my father left school at the age of thirteen and went as clerk to a firm of auctioneers in Liverpool. His schooling therefore was of the briefest.

Height was one of the distinctive features of this family, transmitted to the children from both sides; they were all uncommonly, in the case of the girls unbecomingly, tall and, with the sole exception of my father, uncommonly plain. Three of his sisters, Emily, Susan and Sally, survived into my early middle age; unfortunate creatures, kind though they were their appearance was so grotesque that it is difficult to suppose they could ever have known romance or believed themselves destined for anything but the lifelong spinsterhood which was their lot. Over six feet in height, gaunt and flat-chested, with harsh voices and large hands and feet, Emily and Sally could easily have masqueraded in the clothes of their youngest brother, my Uncle Denton, without the imposture being detected or their prospects in life improved. This leathery-skinned, equine uncle, who outlived the rest of his family, told me that his father was a good-looking man. If so the only photograph of him I ever saw did not do him justice. Be that as it may, if there were good looks about, my father got them all; he was not merely better looking than the rest, he was a strikingly handsome man.

In 1879, when he was sixteen years old and already nearly six feet tall, he ran away to London and joined the Army. I know of no special reasons for this step, reasons stronger than might drive any spirited youth cramped up with a large family in a small cottage on restricted means to go off in search of life and adventure. It is true that his father was something of a disciplinarian ('My old Dad had a very heavy hand. I can feel it still.'), but he respected him and was on good terms with his brothers and sisters. His mother he had scarcely known; she died when he was two years old, after Denton's birth.

He enlisted at Regent's Park Barracks as a private in the Royal Horse Guards, the Blues, giving his age as nearly eighteen. In this regiment he served for three-and-a-half years, of which eighty days were spent campaigning in Egypt, where he took part in the Battle of Tel-el-Kebir. In 1882 he purchased his discharge for £28. Nine months later, July, 1883, he re-enlisted in the Second Life Guards: Trooper Alfred Ackerley. From this regiment he purchased his discharge less than a year later, in 1884, for £18. Throughout his service with these two units he refused all promotion. There was a brief moment in Alexandria when his colonel compelled him to 'take the tabs', and reduced him back to the ranks within twenty-four hours for being carried back to camp by the drunks he had been detailed to bring in. It was an anecdote he liked to recall in later life, as he liked also to recall some of his conquests. The conquests were not, of course, military conquests; to the Battle of Tel-el-Kebir I don't recollect that he ever referred; they were amorous exploits, his own or some crony's, such as how he was almost caught *in flagrante delicto* with his colour-sergeant's young wife. I have forgotten these tales now, but he would sometimes regale me with them in the 'twenties when, the ladies having retired to the drawing-room leaving him and me together, he would circulate the port and brandy and, his Gentleman's cigar in his mouth, reach an unbuttoned stage of mellowness and ease.

The Household Cavalry are a fine body of men, much admired for their magnificent physique and the splendour of their accoutrements, but it will hardly be claimed for them that they are—or at any rate were—refined in their tastes and habits. Conscription and improved rates of pay may have brought some alteration to the scene, but in my father's young days and on into my own, sex and beer and the constant problem of how to obtain these two luxuries in anything like satisfactory measure on almost invisible means—in his day the Queen's shilling—repre-sented the main leisure preoccupation of many guardsmen and troopers. Nor is this surprising. Healthy and vigorous young men, often, like my father, the merest boys, sud-denly transplanted from a comparatively humdrum pro-vincial or country life into a London barrack-room, exercised and trained all day to the bursting point of physical fitness, and let loose in the evening, with little money and large appetites, to prowl about the Monkey Walk in Hyde Park, the pubs, or West End streets, in uniforms of the most conspicuous and sometimes provocative design—it is hardly surprising that their education in the seductions and pleasures of the world should take rapid strides. The tall handsome youth from the village of Rainhill seated with drawn sword upon his charger in Whitehall, arrayed in plumed helmet, glittering cuirass and white buckskin breeches, and gaped at by admiring spectators who sometimes dropped coins into his highly polished top boots, certainly found life very much to his taste. Unhappily my knowledge of that life and of the years that followed is meagre.

At his final discharge he brought away a good conduct badge, a second-class certificate of education, and the War Medal and Bronze Star of the Egyptian Campaign. He brought away two other things, the seeds of success in life and the seeds of death. I will come to the latter in its due place. So far as the former is concerned, something has to be found to account for the transformation of Trooper Alfred Ackerley with his second-class certificate of education and impecunious family background in 1884, into the cultivated, urbane, travelled and polished young man of the world with £2000 a year who picked up my mother on a Channel boat in 1892 and was later to become one of the directors of Elders and Fyffes, fruit merchants, earning £12,000 a year and the title of Banana King when he died.

Four

THE answer lies with two wealthy gentlemen whom my father met in London during his five years of soldiering. How he met them I do not know; so far as my information goes he had no friends in London when he first arrived there in 1879. One of them he must have met soon after his enlistment in the Blues when he was sixteen years old. Of this gentleman I can give only the briefest sketch. His name was Fitzroy Paley Ashmore and he called himself a barrister. He was a friend of Mr Justice Darling, and a married man with four children. My father seldom mentioned him except to remark on occasion that he owed to Ashmore everything he knew. My father wrote a beautiful hand and was a faultless speller, he took a pride in his knowledge of English and never failed to look up in the dictionary the words he did not understand when he was reading. This self-discipline in education, which he often recommended to our inattentive ears, he attributed wholly to Mr Ashmore's training. Yet their friendship was short, this friendship of a rich, cultivated man in his early thirties with an uneducated boy-soldier of sixteen or seventeen, for Ashmore died, aged thirty-seven, in 1883. The whole episode was therefore contained within four years.

Ashmore lived at 18 Radnor Place, Hyde Park, and it seems to have been given out that my father acted as his secretary. His son, Major-General E. B. Ashmore, CB, CMG, MVO, told me, however, that since his father, who had substantial independent means (he died worth £28,000), did no work at all, it was surprising to learn that he needed a secretary. General Ashmore knew nothing about my father (or so he said) and not much about his own who had died when he himself was eleven; what little he did know he was in no mind to praise. His father's only interest in life, said he, was to enjoy himself, gamble and go to parties; he was so unpleasant to his wife that she was more relieved than afflicted to find herself a widow, and all his children, including himself, were terrified of him. But if Mr Ashmore cared not a fig for his wife and children, he took a fancy to my teen-age father and considerable pains to educate him. On August 3, 1882, probably a few days before my father sailed for Egypt, Ashmore drew up a codicil to his will leaving him a legacy of £500, a gift that was to lead to trouble in the end. It was to be held in trust for him by his own father until he reached the age of twenty-one. On October 30, directly after his return from Egypt, he purchased his discharge. Did he go and live at Radnor Place as his benefactor's secretary? I have no information about this period. In the following year, on June 12, Ashmore had a heart attack and died. Three weeks later my father re-enlisted.

The educational and refining processes begun upon him by Mr Ashmore were continued by the Count James Francis de Gallatin, my father's other wealthy friend. Whether he was met through Ashmore or independently I don't know, but he now supplied Ashmore's place in my father's young life. A Count of the Holy Roman Empire and descendant of a famous Swiss-American family, he kept two establishments, one in Mount Street, Berkeley

Square, the other in Old Windsor, a house called The
Hermitage. Doubtless considerably altered it still stands.
He was a bachelor, aged thirty-one, and lived with his
mother. He too took to my soldier father in a big way;
soon, indeed, he could hardly bear to let him out of his
sight.

I have said that my father twice purchased his discharge
from the Army; it is more probable that he was bought out,
first by Mr Ashmore and now, in February, 1884, through
the persuasions and help of the Count de Gallatin. The indi-
cations are that by this time they were close friends and that
family introductions, my father to Mme de Gallatin in
Mount Street and Old Windsor, the Count to my father's
family in Rainhill, had been established. Two more basic
reasons for this second and sudden retirement of my father
from the Army suggest themselves: his old father had been
taken ill with cancer of the tongue, and in the April of that
year my father would be twenty-one and come into possession of his legacy. He returned to Liverpool and took a job
as traveller in the business of his brother-in-law, John
Graham, a wine merchant. His legacy fell due to him on his
birthday, April 1; he did not spend it but 'lent' it to the
Count. Other records say he gave it to the Count to keep
for him. De Gallatin was a generous man as we shall see
(a little later he was to take trouble to help Denton gain a
foothold in South Africa by introducing him to titled and
influential people), and one can hazard a guess at the actual
circumstances of this transaction, for he undertook to pay
my father the large interest of 20% on the 'loan'. It is the
kind of thing a rich man might do to help out, as delicately
as possible, a friend of whom he was fond and who was

short of cash. This £100 a year and whatever commission he earned from his travelling was all the money my father had.

Early in the following year, 1885, old Mr Ackerley died. The doctors had gradually cut away most of his tongue (radium treatment was not then known), but the cancer had moved to his stomach. At this time occurred another important event in my father's life: he met and quickly palled up with a local youth named Arthur Stockley, aged twenty.

In the spring of that same year de Gallatin, perhaps to be near my father, rented for the summer a furnished house in the district in New Brighton, Cheshire, and invited him to stay and bring with him any friend he liked. My father took Stockley. There was a fourth member of the party, a friend of the Count's, another very handsome youth named Dudley Sykes, of whom I know nothing. In the words of Stockley he was 'very good-looking, charming and quite harmless and never did a day's work in his life'. He was not a guardsman. I have included a photograph of this quartet, taken in this time and place. They are sitting in the garden grouped beneath a tree on a tatty lion-skin rug spread on the grass. Bold and roving-eyed* Mr Sykes is bare-headed, the rest wear boaters. Excepting Stockley all sport moustaches in the custom of the period; the Count's is particularly heavy. They are dressed in open-necked shirts and their flannel trousers are supported by dark cummerbunds. A shaggy dog with a beard like Kruger's lolls among them. The Count was fond of dogs.

*There are two photographs. In the one I have selected Mr Sykes' eyes are invisible.

Behind them, along the sill of an open window, potted plants are ranged. Would that I had been able to peep and eavesdrop through that window and discover their secrets, if any. But I was not yet born.

What did they do? Stockley, who, I feel sure, had no interesting secrets, went off to Liverpool every day on whatever business he was engaged in, perhaps the fruit trade in which he was to end; my father, still in the employ of Graham, doubtless travelled locally too, trying to gain sales; young Mr Sykes idled about. In the evenings and at weekends they came together, bathed, played poker and whatever athletic games were available to them (I have a photo of my father and Stockley sparring in boxing gloves). The Count, who paid for everything ('We lived there in considerable luxury,' writes Stockley), had a smart dog-cart and cob, in which they probably rattled about. Mme de Gallatin was not present, and Stockley says they had no female society of any sort. They 'created quite a sensation', he says. The local residents were not used to, were suspicious and perhaps jealous of, so strange a household which contained a rich foreign nobleman with rather poppy eyes and two strikingly handsome young men, and some busybody wrote to Stockley's mother in Worcestershire to warn her that her son was rapidly 'being ruined by an adventurer and his *confrères*'. 'However, this did not trouble me, as I knew it was entirely untrue.'

My father, aged twenty-two, seated in a chair, looks very attractive, more solid and serious than Mr Sykes with his rather theatrical d'Artagnan face, and the Count by now was clearly bowled over by him. When the party broke up he did not want my father to return to Liverpool; unable to prevent this, he went with him and accompanied him upon his commercial errands. I have a dashingly punctuated letter of his to Stockley, from the Queen's Hotel, Stockton, written on a Sunday in November, 1885:

'Here we are at the most awful place I have ever seen— Durham was quite charming and I was sorry we did not stop there for Sunday. We get on like a house on fire, the only thing is poor old Roger rather worries as he cannot get any orders—there is no business doing at all—I enclose a cheque for £8.8s. Will you kindly pay Roger's dues at the Racquet Club—I believe the sum is £7.17s.6. Pay *yourself* the 2/6 you paid for me for the cab last Sunday—the balance will do when we meet. I had a full account of my good fortune from Morley—I knew there was a large property in America but I did not know it was so much. The truth is I don't bother myself much about my affairs. I wish you were with us as it is most amusing. Awfully cheap travelling and we have met very decent people—at Durham I had a pal who was very civil to us. We will be back (D.V. as my mother says) on Friday night. It is now 1.45 and we have just come down to breakfast.'

Clearly my father's job was proving unremunerative and it was not long before a more congenial occupation was suggested. Close to The Hermitage, the Count's cottage, as he called it, in Old Windsor, was a disused farm, known as The Cell Farm, which the Count rented for stabling and grazing his ponies. The suggestion now was that this small farm might be stocked with more ponies to become a pony farm and run by my father as a business concern: with his cavalryman's experience he was knowledgeable about horses. It seems that he was staying with the de Gallatins at The Hermitage when this idea was conceived, that it originated in the mind of a third person, and that it was proposed by my father to the Count. It was, of course, instantly agreed to, for it gave de Gallatin his heart's desire, my father's permanent companionship. Stockley says that he thereupon bought The Cell Farm for my father, who took up residence there and at The Hermitage in 1886. Soon afterwards he fell ill. I don't know the nature of his complaint, but it must have been something serious, for the de Gallatins took him abroad to Italy for six months to convalesce. I have a letter from my father to Stockley, written from Rome on the Count's coroneted notepaper and dated November 2, 1886. Like most of the few letters I use—the only ones I possess—it is rather a bore, but parts of it are relevant to the rest of this sad story:

'We have had a very good time, and shall be settling down at the Villa Rocca Bella, Naples, about next Friday, for which mercy thank the pigs, as the continual packing and unpacking is awful. G. won about £300 at Monte Carlo, you never saw such a lucky beggar in your life and you never saw such an unlucky beggar as yours truly, my past sins were all heaped on my head, as every piece I put down was promptly raked in by the croupier. . . . If all present arrangements hold good, I shall come back by sea straight from Naples to Liverpool about April next and go on to Ireland from there to see about the ponies of which there are about 9 for me to break in and sell so if you hear of anyone in want of a good one, let me know.

You might let me have any news that would interest a poor invalid, (for I am still under the doctor) write to Naples.'

De Gallatin accompanied him to Ireland in the spring of the following year and bought ten ponies for £50 at Fairhill Fair, Galway. Until they could be transported to England they were left on the estate of a Lord Wallscourt, where their keep and the grooms' wages had to be defrayed. By the time they were all brought over and assembled at The Cell Farm they had cost the Count another £200.

Thereafter matters proceeded quietly for some eighteen months, my father living with and, presumably, largely on, the de Gallatins, breaking in and selling ponies at no great profit, riding in point-to-point races and taking part in the social life of Windsor. To Stockley, July 2, 1887:

'I have suddenly wakened up to the idea that you must be under the erroneous impression that I am an awful bounder not to have answered your letter before, but really I must assure you with all the veracity of a Roger that when your letter came I was in throes of learning my part and let me also assure [you] a very important part in some theatricals which we played for two nights on the stage of the Theatre Royal, Windsor, to crowded houses, if you don't believe me look up *The Times* of that date which speaks of my marvellous talent etc. etc. I had several invitations from various young damsels to come to their boudoirs for supper etc. which with my natural modesty I refused, from high moral motives.

Joking apart, old chap, I am awfully ashamed of myself.
. . . Let me know if you are coming up, Gallatin is
awfully down on me for not writing before. . . .'

Over a year later, in September, 1888, de Gallatin, who
and been bitten in the leg by a fly and laid up for a month,
wrote to Stockley: 'Poor old Roger is as good-tempered
and satisfied as ever—we jog on here in our own quiet way—
and I think it suits us all—The Cottage is looking awfully
neat now and I like it so much that I am going to build some
more rooms. . . .' But good temper and the happy domestic
scene were not to last much longer; before the year's end
Miss Louise Burckhardt came over from Paris to stay with
the de Gallatins. Of this young lady I know scarcely anything. She was of wealthy parentage and Swiss. Arthur
Stockley informed me that she came over with some prospect of marrying the Count, to whom she was said to be
related; but Stockley's old-age memory was far from
accurate, as I shall have occasion to show later; moreover
he was no longer in England at this critical time, he sailed
for Grand Canary in November to learn about the fruit
trade and was not to meet my father again until 1892, four
years later, though they continued to correspond. He never
met Miss Burckhardt at all.

Whatever the truth of the matter, finding at The Hermitage handsome young Mr Ackerley, Louise engaged herself to him. It was quickly done. They announced their
engagement before the turn of the year and expressed their
desire to leave. The Count was said by everyone who knew
him to be an extremely jealous man; he was deeply upset and
I expect he behaved badly. However, whether he was upset

at losing Louise or at losing my father the reader must decide for himself. I can provide no details of the sequence of events, but I can provide a letter from which the emotional atmosphere, at least, may be gauged. It is from Mme de Gallatin to Stockley in Grand Canary. It is undated, but internal evidence shows that it was written after the New Year. Dashed off (one can see whence the Count derived his punctuation) in an overwrought state of mind, it is not easy to decipher, but I give it, at something of an occasional guess, in full:

'I enclose these few lines marked private for *you alone* and that is to say how deeply I *mourn* for my poor son in his grief and suffering through the *unheard of* and *incredible* treatment he has received from Roger. I write to thank you with all my heart for your *loyalty* and *affection* for my poor boy—No one *but* I knows how he *suffers* he says *nothing* and tries to brave it and not to let me nor anyone see what he feels—but I tell you *frankly* that his heart is broken and that he never has been the same and never will be—and my suffering for him is so great that I am old, and it is breaking me down. Roger came to us and took the place of my dear son I lost [the Count's brother], he was James' brother and James and I treated him as a son and brother and gave him all our affection and devotion. James had such faith in him, and often said to me Mother if I die before you Roger will take care of you, be good to you, for *he* can always be relied on—James trusted in him as *almost* in his God—and to come to a house where he had been *cherished* at *five* o'clock one afternoon, pack up his traps and leave at *eight* that evening *forever* without a word of warning nearly killed us both—James has *never* been able to remain at home since—I *see* it he *cannot*—he says everything is so connected with Roger that he suffers too much—He has brought on James' ill health for *entre nous strictly* James's heart is very weak and the doctor says that he must have had a severe shock during the New Year to his heart!

I would never have opposed Roger leaving us to try and do better or to *work* but it was the *way* he left us and his *treachery* and all the underhand things he has done— and *more than all* his fearful ingratitude—he has behaved like a coward and a *sneak*— for *I* do not mince matters where justice demands me to speak frankly—He has not moral courage enough to be a friend! And he has sacrificed his best friend and a noble heart for *Money*! This is what I think of him. I forgive him but I can never think well of him again. My son will never be the same.

I thank you with all my heart for being so true to my son and he and I feel it deeply and will always do anything in our power for you.

If Roger had remained with us and *worked* and really tried to manage his ponies—James and I would have given him up The Cell Farm altogether and he would have been a small farmer and at the same time had his ponies— but he has given up his best friends.'

This letter does not read to me like the indignation of a devoted mother who has had a prospective daughter-in-law filched away; the loss the Count suffered was not the loss of a bride. The sequence of events is obscure, but it would appear that after leaving Old Windsor with his fiancée, my father returned at some moment later, perhaps surreptitiously, and cleared his belongings out of The Cell Farm. His subsequent movements are not known to me. An aunt of his by marriage, Aunt Maggie as we knew her as children, the widow of his father's brother Charles, who had been a successful skin-and-hide merchant in Buenos Aires, came to settle in Hampstead in 1886; she is said to have been very fond of my father and it may be that the runaway couple took refuge with her. He certainly brought Louise up to Cheshire to meet his family, for I have a photograph of them together taken in New Brighton. And doubtless she took him to Paris to meet her parents. They were married, nearly a year later, in the Church of the Holy Trinity, Avenue de l'Alma, on September 25, 1889. Then they honeymooned through Europe. From the Hotel la Luna, Venice, my father wrote to Arthur Stockley on October 13 of that year:

'Dear old chap,
  I hear that you are expected in England shortly, to be married and done for; having just gone through that most interesting ceremony myself and having now nearly three weeks experience of married life, I feel competent to assure you that you could not do better, and at the same time to wish you just as much happiness and joy and as nice a partner as I have got; she reads this and is now patting my cheek.
  Having seen your photograph so often and having heard of you as well, always as a good pal, she wishes to add her good wishes to mine. . . . We have had a jolly tour for our honeymoon, Basle, Lucerne, Flüelen,

Lugano, Milan, Venice and back by way of Turin and Lyons to Paris.

We shall spend the winter at Wiesbaden in Germany, where I am going to try to master that gutteral language.

My address in Paris is 64 Boulevard de Courcelles and I shall hope to find a letter there from you when I arrive on Friday next.

The weather here has not been very propitious, but weather and mosquitoes and fleas all of which are here in plenty don't matter as long as you are in love, which I hear is the case with you, all the way from Bombay.

Now, old chap, do write me just a few lines and let me know when and where and how and believe that I am the same old humbug though I am married, at least so my wife says.'

Not long afterwards Louise was taken ill—some tubercular trouble, I think—and eighteen months later, early in 1892, she died.

Five

1892: we return to that year which was to be of such consequence to myself and was also, I suppose, one of the most
momentous in my father's life, containing as it did so many
of the major events that were to shape his destiny. He lost a
wife at the beginning of it and met a mistress, my mother,
towards the end. In it too Stockley reappeared and engaged
him in the fruit trade in which he was to make his fortune.
And in it occurred a sombre episode which I find both
puzzling and distasteful: Mr Ashmore's legacy reared its
ugly head. In July a civil action between my father and the
Count de Gallatin was tried in the Law Courts before Mr
Justice Collins.

When I first projected this memoir some thirty years ago
and was seeking information about my father's early life, I
applied to Arthur Stockley, his partner and lifelong friend,
then a man of seventy-three. One of his letters to me
contains the following sentence: 'I suppose he [de Gallatin]
could not help his intensely jealous nature, but there was no
cause for him bringing an action against your father over
The Cell Farm just because of the Louise incident; however he lost the action and had to pay the costs, which
made him quite frantic.' But the case, I afterwards
discovered, is reported at some length in *The Times* of
July 21, 1892; my father was the plaintiff and must therefore have brought the action and judgment was given
for the defendant (the Count). It is true he was saddled

with the costs; it seems the only accuracy in Stockley's statement.

The action was brought by my father to recover the £500 which he had lent to de Gallatin eight years previously. The Count admitted the loan but asserted that the suggestion to start the pony farm had come from my father, who had proposed that the £500 should be used for running and stocking it. He himself had agreed to this and to transact the business on my father's behalf. He had had no share in the profits of the farm and claimed that he had told my father, when the latter left him in November, 1888, that he had spent more than £500 on it, that they had better cry quits, and that my father had agreed. Some unpleasantness then arose: after the marriage my father's relatives began to enquire what had become of his legacy. The Count said that he then proposed to treat the losses at the pony farm as his own and to repay the £500. A correspondence ensued in which he wrote to my father to ask what should be done with the remaining ponies. My father instructed him to send them to Tattersall's. Two of them fetched £42, the unbroken ones £14. Complaints kept coming from my father's relatives and he, the Count, had then decided not to repay the £500. Instead he counter-claimed for over £600 as representing his own expenses over the farm. He did not now insist upon his counter-claim. No accounts had been kept, but cheques paid by him to my father were available and the correspondence showed that my father had looked upon the farm as his own.

My father in his evidence stated that before they went to Ireland nothing had been said about buying ponies. They were bought, he said, simply to give him something to do in looking after them. All the arrangements were made by the Count. He himself broke and sold the ponies as they came along, paid wages out of the money received, kept some himself and, if the settlement was by cheque, paid it into the Count's banking account. The latter had never put forward any claim for expenses and it was untrue to say that they had agreed to cry quits. My father had made repeated application for the repayment of his £500.

Mr Justice Collins, delivering judgment, said that the plaintiff was a person for whom the defendant had strong feelings of affection, giving him free quarters and providing him with money for some years, at a time also when he was paying interest on the loan. It was clear that at one time the defendant had wished to pay off the loan, for which he was giving heavy interest. On the one hand the plaintiff had lent £500, on the other he had free quarters and pocket money from the defendant. The question was whether the ponies were the property of the plaintiff or the defendant: the admission of counsel had narrowed the case down to that issue. After looking at the correspondence between the parties there could be only one answer. The defendant wrote to the plaintiff asking for instructions about the unsold ponies, and the plaintiff provided those instructions. How could it be said that it was necessary for the plaintiff to authorise the defendant to sell the ponies unless they were his? The plaintiff also admitted that when he sold the ponies he applied the proceeds to his own purposes. Judgment must be given for the defendant with costs.

I confess to finding almost every aspect of this wretched dispute obscure and can only hazard a guess at the truth of the matter. From my own experience of life and my knowledge of my father's character in later years, I would say that his version was substantially true. During his four-year association with de Gallatin he was in his early twenties, and if it occurs to readers of this memoir that even when Banana King he seemed somewhat lacking in business sense, he was unlikely to have had much then. Though easy-going, as I knew him, he was also of an independent and obstinate nature, and he had two favourite words of contempt for idle and parasitic people: 'loafer' and 'sponger'. We have already noted the Count's failure to detain him in idleness in New Brighton. The pony farm was not much of a job, but it had the appearance of one and the extra attraction of being the only kind of work which this young ex-cavalryman understood and enjoyed. Disguised as a profitable enterprise, it was little more than a toy for him to play with; behind the scene the Count was virtually keeping him: in his letters his reference to him as a pony-farmer is the same as his reference to him as a failing wine-salesman, 'poor old Roger'—an affectionate, somewhat patronising phrase. In later life my father would not have cared to be patronised, and if patronage did not irk him a little then, it was, I believe, simply because of his legacy. This legacy, invested in the Count, must have stood for him as a symbol of prime importance, a symbol of independence and self-esteem; it enabled him to loaf and sponge in a dignified manner, it saved his face. Whatever proposals or suggestions he may have made in the initial transactions for the application of this nest-egg towards the costs of the farm were probably more formal and graceful than sincere; how could he suppose that his devoted and generous friend, who always paid for everything for everyone and had ample means to do so, would take his pretty offer seriously? Nor do I believe that the Count did take it seriously, until the bust-up; he did not need or want my father's money (he got through three fortunes in a lifetime, Stockley says), he wanted only my father; it must surely have been plain to him that his own best interest lay not in spending his young friend's capital but in preserving it; doubtless he eagerly agreed to whatever proposals were made, so long as they gained him my father's company.

That obtained, I imagine that expenses were seldom discussed between them; from the doting Count's point of view the less said about them the better; unbusinesslike himself ('The truth is I don't bother myself much about my affairs,' he had said in that letter to Stockley) but a lavish spender, he paid readily and unobtrusively for everything without counting the cost, and far from wishing to break into his young friend's nest-egg, he had at one time tried, it seems—I wonder when and why—to pay the loan of it off. All this while the sun shone and 'We jog along here in our own quiet way—and I think it suits us all'; when the clouds gathered, the scene changed, and the word most stressed in Mme de Gallatin's charges against my father is 'ingratitude', saddest of words.

If my father's capital sum was important to him for the preservation of his dignity in Old Windsor, its monetary value could never have been greater than when he wished to leave with Louise. It must have been humiliating for him to be paid for all along the line by his fiancée (as I assume happened, unless Aunt Maggie or some other friend lent him money), rich though her parents might be, and be presented penniless to them. In the days when I knew him one could not take a lady out to dine, even a relative, without giving her champagne; it wasn't 'done'. It was now, however, that the mortified Count totted up a bill that had never existed. I find it hard to believe that in such a situation my father would have agreed to cry quits—unless in the kind of proud and angry way in which one might say, 'Put it where the monkey put the nuts!' Cash was then too important to him. It is difficult to avoid the conclusion that if he behaved ruthlessly, the Count behaved spitefully; had he restored to my father at their parting even a portion of the loan the dreary suit might never have been brought.

But all this is of less interest to me than the question: Why did my father bring the matter to court? By the time it was heard, four years had elapsed and he was a widower with a handsome allowance of £2000 a year. When were the wheels of justice set in motion? Some time after the marriage in September, 1889, it seems. They are reputed to turn slowly; they can also be stayed and matters settled out of court. After all, whatever unpleasantness had arisen at his parting from the de Gallatins (and the scene may well have been pretty nasty) they had been devoted friends to him and he was deeply in their debt for much love, care, and kindness. There had been plenty of time to calm down and reflect on this. On the face of it it seems a mean thing to have done, and my father as I knew him was not mean, though he could be stubborn and relentless, as we shall see. Who were these relatives who began annoying the Count a year after the event? Except for Aunt Maggie and, perhaps, John Graham, they were all down at heel: my father entirely supported his three spinster sisters, Susan, Sally, and

Emily, in their declining years until they died. Had he perhaps promised the indigent part of his family the legacy if they could extract it? Did they keep the dispute going while he was abroad? Could they have filed the suit in his absence? Even so, why did he allow it to come to court? Stockley says that the judge ticked him off, remarking that he had not 'behaved well'. Nothing of this appears in *The Times* report and no official transcript of the trial survives. Or did the Count drive him to law by forcing on his counter-claim? There is a fragment of evidence to which we shall come which shows de Gallatin to have been of a vindictive nature: Stockley himself, who liked and continued friendly with him in spite of everything, uses the word. It may therefore be that the Count pushed the matter to an issue. Is that why he got saddled with the costs?

At any rate, considering the whole sad affair in its obscurity as objectively as one can, it looks like one of those bitter lessons so many of us learn who try to buy the human heart with cash. That it taught the poor Count a lesson I have reason to doubt; I am convinced that it taught one to my father. Never while I knew him thirty years later would he accept hospitality if he could help it. He dispensed it, and as lavishly as the Count; he would take none in return. I used to think it selfish of him never to allow others, however much they begged and however comfortable their means, the pleasure of treating him in return for all his treats. Constant visitors to our house and table, people who stayed with us, often for weeks, and enjoyed the delights of his cellar and my mother's five-course meals, frequent guests of his at his favourite restaurant, Romano's in the Strand, all tried to secure him to themselves as a guest, but he would have none of it. Occasionally, I remember, he seemed cornered and we dined out at the compelling invitation of some prosperous friend; but always, at the end of the meal, my father managed, by some ruse, to get hold of the bill and settle it himself, even though this involved unseemly scuffles over the wretched piece of paper, merely chuckling at the embarrassed or disappointed expostulations that followed. It seemed as though it made him positively uncomfortable to be paid for, or even to receive gifts of any value: when I was a schoolboy and a wealthy friend of his, Captain Bacon, Chairman of the Manchester Ship Canal, sent me a cheque for £100 for some now forgotten literary project I had in hand—my school magazine perhaps—and wrote, 'Put it in your own pocket if you don't need it all for that', my father made me return the cheque. Yet if he disliked being under obligations to others, he was not above bribing his own way in life and, like any de Gallatin, expecting gratitude and loyalty in return for generosity. When we dined out or stayed in a hotel, head waiters would be liberally tipped beforehand to ensure that we received special attention, every privilege; my father would actually say, 'There, see that I am well looked after and I shan't forget you later.'

Bribery did not always work; the displeasure, as in de Gallatin's case, was then severe. It was one of my father's boasts that his employees in Elders and Fyffes never struck, their needs were always anticipated and provided for, their wages raised before the point of demand was reached. The firm was therefore regarded as a happy family, and my father was godfather to innumerable staff children, none of whose birthdays and the silver christening mugs he bestowed, he ever forgot. But in the General Strike a shocking thing happened; some of these happy employees, the transport side, the van-drivers, were either obliged or felt obliged out of another loyalty, to their unions, to join the strike. They lost their jobs, and out of this situation trouble brewed also for two other persons, a taxi-driver and myself. My father had a pet taxi-driver named Mickey. I never saw this man, but there was something about him that took my father's fancy. His rank was at Waterloo Station which my father used for his Bow Street office, coming up from Richmond where we lived, and in course of time a sort of friendship grew up between them so that Mickey became his special driver. Refusing other fares he would meet my father's regular train and drive him to his office. Soon he was calling at the office in the evening to drive him back to Waterloo, sometimes right down to Richmond; whenever a taxi was wanted by my father for anything it had to be Mickey's if possible. This man was a character, my father delighted in him, gave him handsome tips and presents, such as hands of bananas, sent presents to his family and talked about him so much that we used to ask after him, as though he were a pet dog. But in the strike his union called him out, and he met my father's train no more until the dispute was settled. My father never spoke to him again. Walking past him at Waterloo without a look, he would enter another taxi. Poor Mickey was genuinely upset; he had, I think, formed a personal attachment to my father. He called a number of times at the Bow Street office but was refused admittance. He even drove all the way down to Richmond one day to ask my mother to intercede for him. She did, but my father remained unmoved. The man had let him down and was never seen or heard of again. Some months later, suddenly at table, following some light remark I happened to make, my father unleashed upon my startled head a perfect torrent of reproach for not having put myself and my car at his service in his time of need as the sons of his colleagues, he said, had done for their fathers. It was the most shocking and unique experience for me, this violent discharge of pent-up grievances which he had been nursing for so long. The notion of helping him had never crossed my mind. Had I realised what was going on in his head, that he was silently waiting and hoping for my offer and suffering in his pride because it did not come, I would gladly have helped him, though I was a socialist at the time and my sympathies lay with the strikers. I said I was very sorry but I hadn't thought, to which he retorted, No, of course I hadn't thought, he realised that, I never did think of anyone but myself, I was just as selfish and ungrateful as my sister Nancy, and he did not know what he had done to deserve two such selfish and ungrateful children. What he had done we ourselves did not then know, but we found out later.

Returning now to the legal dispute, how interesting is Stockley's reversal of the facts forty-six years later. He was, I believe, an honest man, as this world and the business world go, of a rigid moral code, severe and self-righteous (his standards of human perfection were King George the Fifth and Rudyard Kipling): perhaps the final order of his loyalties affected his beliefs. Or did my father contrive, out of uneasiness, to throw dust in his eyes, as he seems to have done in another matter to which we shall soon come? It is possible that Stockley was not back in England when the action was judged in July, and heard of it only afterwards from my father, whom he ran into by chance at the Tivoli. But the margin must have been slight, for both these events took place in that same month. At any rate he had no part in the legal proceedings and tried to keep out of the squabble. He was friendly with both de Gallatin and my father; the former had been best man at his wedding three years previously and godfather to his son and heir. But he was not to be allowed to sit on the fence. He was busy inaugurating in Covent Garden the banana business which, starting in an almost costermongerish way, was to become Elders and Fyffes, and my father, bored with idleness, asked if he could come in as 'office boy'. He was accepted. But when de Gallatin heard that he was to be employed by Stockley, he wrote angrily to the latter to say he 'must choose between them' who was his friend. 'It was a ridiculous request,' says Stockley, 'and I did not hesitate.' When Mme de Gallatin was dying some years later she summoned him and he went ('I never blamed her as she was devoted to G., and one can understand a mother's unreasonableness'), but the Count was never again seen by him or by my father and disappears out of their story to arise later as a ghost in my own.

The year 1892, therefore, was a momentous one in my father's life; in it he lost a wife, gained a job which was to make his name and fortune, and picked up my mother on a Channel boat. She was not, as we have seen, his first conquest, nor was she to be his last, and it may therefore be permissible to wonder how long the affair would have continued had not an accident occurred.

Six

My elder brother Peter was the accident. 'Your father happened to have run out of french letters that day,' remarked my Aunt Bunny with her Saloon Bar laugh, and I have for some time been aware that if I am to get this history even approximately straight I must somehow steer a course between my aunt's rabelaisian humour, my mother's romanticism, and the mutual jealousies of both. Nevertheless my brother was neither intended nor wanted and efforts, probably of an amateur kind, were made to prevent his arrival. My mother was thirty-one years old at this time and working on the stage, a more respectable stage than the one Aunt Bunny was to reach, known indeed as the 'legitimate' stage (she was a recruit of Sir Herbert Beerbohm Tree): this is not however to suggest that she should therefore have known better. Doctors were confidentially consulted, various homely remedies prescribed, and all manner of purges, nostrums, and bodily exercises employed to bring about a miscarriage. But my brother was not to be quenched. Nevertheless he did not survive unscathed. He emerged prematurely, a seven-month child and breach delivery, double-ruptured, jaundiced and black in the face, presenting altogether so wretched and puny an appearance with his head sunk between his shoulders like a tortoise that the doctor in attendance remarked, more prophetically, it may be thought, than he realised, 'Seems hardly worth saving.' This event occurred on October 6, 1895, in

Melcombe Place, Marylebone, where my mother's family were then living. Mr Ackerley then concealed Netta Aylward (my mother's maiden name) and the child at 4 Warminster Road, Herne Hill, in care of his grandmother and of a faithful housekeeper of his named Sarah.

If Arthur Stockley's memory is to be trusted my father withheld from him, then and always, the truth of his dealings with my mother, for up to the end of his life Stockley believed that they had been married at the Marylebone Register Office before my brother was born. 'The marriage was kept secret,' he wrote me, 'as your father did not want old B. [Burckhardt] to know of it.' Secrecy, for some reason, was maintained by both of them, in spite of the death of 'old B.', for nearly ten years; it was not until about 1904 that it came out accidentally that my father had a 'wife' and three children living up in Cheshire, news which greatly puzzled and displeased some of his business friends, who wondered why they had been kept in the dark.

This book is not about my brother, but in connection with him my own character and story develop and his subsequent history must be briefly sketched. Fed at first through a quill, for he could not suck, and wrapped in cotton wool soaked in cod-liver oil, this flickering life was gradually brought, mainly by the unremitting care and skill of my grandmother, through a sickly childhood, to become in time a tall, thin, dark, rather sallow youth of a lively and good-tempered disposition. He liked practical jokes and all forms of buffoonery, was good at playing cricket and the bones, had a charming natural tenor voice and a leaning towards the stage: he collected pictures of Henry Irving and Beerbohm Tree and was always acting and dressing up.

This was in my mother's tradition, but the paternal influence was stronger and he was training to enter our father's business when the 1914 war broke out. This brought in the paternal example again : my mother said, 'Thank Heaven my boys are too young to join up,' and we offered ourselves to the Army at once. I was accepted; my brother, who had been obliged to wear a truss throughout his life, was rejected. The patriotic fervour of the time, which looks in retrospect so idiotic, was strong; he was not a chap to be left out of drama of any kind and resolved to have his rupture corrected by an operation. To this decision he was encouraged by our family doctor, a handsome, dandified sportsman named Harry Wadd, who took my brother along with him to hospital one day to watch the same operation performed upon someone else before he underwent it himself—an invitation I myself would certainly have refused. But there was, I think, in my brother a streak of bravado, inherited from my father, which I did not possess; though was it not to carry it too far to dress up for the benefit of the specialist who was engaged to perform the operation? That eminent and busy man was somewhat taken aback to find in the nursing home not the youth he was expecting but a grotesque bearded tramp with a red cardboard nose and huge *papiermâché* feet. However, the operation was successful and some time later my brother was accepted by the Army. In 1918, just before the Armistice, he was killed by a whizz-bang. My parents were married in the following year.

Possibly this sequence of events, this brief potted biography, which actually spread itself over nearly a quarter of a century, did not present itself to them in the crude light in which I have sketched it in; but I feel that to my father at least it may have done so, and that although Aunt Bunny's intervention on my mother's behalf at Pegwell Bay may have been the determining card which won the belated day, the true cause of the marriage lay in some deep, sad desire to make amends. Be that as it may, however little my father welcomed my brother when he came, he lost his favourite son when he died. Peter approximated far closer than I did to the paternal image, a chip of the old block, and was already set to fulfill my father's cherished ambitions: he would have married and, perhaps, provided grand-children (he was already courting several girls before he died and my father was fond of children), and he would have entered the banana business. Finally, it may be added, he would not have written this book. He was, in fact, all the things that I was not, though we got along together per-fectly well.

He was fond and proud of me and thought me a being far superior to himself, a genius. We never quarrelled over anything that I can recall, and in all our seventeen or eighteen years together I remember only two occasions when he displayed anger with me, both times for moaning. The first time, which I can relate here, was when I was twelve years old and had a pain in my bowels which the doctors could not for some time diagnose. It was a bad pain, indeed it almost killed me, for it ended in an opera-tion for peritonitis, and I lay moaning in bed day after day for I don't remember how long while doctors came and stuck their fingers up my bottom but did not reach my pain. It was the sound of my moaning that my brother could not stand, and one day he shouted at me for God's sake to shut up, I was upsetting the whole house, said he, and even if I did have a pain there was no reason to kick up such an infernal shindy about it. I was so startled by this heartless attack upon me, for he had never spoken to me in such a way before, that I stopped moaning at once and found he was perfectly right, I did not need to be moaning at all; I had got into the habit of it, I suppose, and it had turned into a kind of self-pitying croon. He apologised afterwards; but later still when he himself lay in the agony of a mastoid he did not utter a sound. He belonged in this respect upon my father's proud 'stiff upper lip' side: 'I hope I can bear a little pain with the best of 'em.' Of this I shall have more to say later, but one other revolting instance of it may be recorded here. From sculling on the river at Richmond where we lived, my brother developed blisters on the palm of one hand, and my father, in whom the original guardsman persisted, told him that the best way to harden blisters was to rub one's own urine into them. This barrack-room remedy resulted in a badly poisoned hand, the whole of the palm oozed with pus. Dr Wadd was summoned and said, 'You can bear a spot of pain, Pete old lad, can't you, or do you want an anaesthetic?' I myself would firmly have demanded an anaesthetic, total if possible, local (if invented then) at least, whatever the expression on my father's face might have been, but my brother said, 'Go ahead.' Wadd then borrowed a pair of scissors from my mother and slit the whole puffed-up palm across. My brother did utter a gasp, turned green and almost fainted; but it was what my father would have called a 'jolly good show'.

My brother was deservedly popular wherever he went, on account of his good nature and his entertainment value,

the versatility of his histrionic talent and his readiness to
display it. Besides his skill with the bones and his true tenor
voice, which was later to keep audiences of soldiers spell-
bound with such songs as 'The Trumpeter', 'Soldier Boy',
'The Mountains of Mourne', and 'Where'er You Walk',
he was a good tap-dancer and a natural comedian. He would,
I think, have been wasted in my father's business. A few
physical details return to my memory: his straight dark
brows that almost met, his narrow palate and weak over-
crowded teeth, the brownish stain round his loins from the
leather of his truss when he took it off to go to the baths at
school, the yellow mark just above the cleft of his thin
white buttocks where the wash-leather pad rested, and his
abnormally long dark cock, longer than my own or any
other I had seen. I remember feeling rather ashamed of it
when we went to the baths together, and wondered how he
could expose it as he did with such seeming indifference
and what the other boys must think. Unspectacular though
my own was I always shielded it modestly from view with
my towel, like a Japanese. I recollect that I had a feeling of
distaste for his thin sallow body, and believe that he had no
such unfriendly thoughts about mine, which was always
erupting in cysts and boils.

Having been sent to school two years in advance of me,
owing to my peritonitis, thereby paving a pleasanter way
for me by being there to welcome and protect me when I
came, for no boys held me down on my back and spat or
poured ink into my mouth as they had done with him, he
left a year earlier than I and went to Germany to learn the
language in preparation for my father's business. His return thence, just before the outbreak of war, impressed upon

my memory his first appearance as a man. He was smoking one of my father's Gentleman cigars and wearing an Edward VII grey felt hat, a heavy reddish-purple overcoat with a belt, patent leather shoes and a monocle. He carried a slender cane like Charlie Chaplin and was beginning to spot round the mouth. I thought he looked an awful ass and rather a cad; not of course foreseeing that in a few years' time I myself might be sighted in London dressed in a voluminous black carabiniero's cloak, cast over one shoulder in the Byronic manner, and trailed by children calling out rude remarks.

After that I remember nothing more about my brother until our last melodramatic meeting. This was in a dugout in France, in a ditch called the Boom Ravine.

Seven

BECAUSE of his rupture my brother entered the war a good deal later than I. He was posted to a battalion of the Northumberland Fusiliers. This unit, however, seemed stuck in England, and my brother, chafing to 'do his bit', got himself transferred to my battalion, the 8th East Surreys, in which I had been serving in France since the summer of 1915. He did not join me there until the Christmas of 1916, after my return from England where I had spent a few months recuperating from wounds. By this time, although he was my senior in age, I was his senior in rank, a captain and company commander, while he was still a second lieutenant in charge of a platoon. He therefore had to salute me, which he did gladly and conscientiously. Let me not appear to boast however; my promotion was not due to any military proficiency I possessed or any distinctions gained, but simply to the fact that most of the other officers in my battalion had been killed on July 1, 1916, the action in which I received my wounds.

These wounds of mine are not without interest, at any rate to me. They showed me something which I was to notice often again in my character, that I have a fairly well-developed instinct for self-preservation, both physical and moral. If the old campaigner of Tel-el-Kebir had known as much about my wounds as I did, what would he have thought of me? The Battle of the Somme, Sir Douglas Haig's masterly operation, has often been described. This vast, full-scale attack was prepared for by an incessant bombardment of the German lines, prolonged over many days and so heavy that, we were told, all resistance would be crushed, the enemy wire destroyed, their trenches flattened, and such Germans as survived reduced to a state of gibbering imbecility. It would be, for us, a walk-over. Very different was our reception. The air, when we at last went over the top in broad daylight, positively hummed, buzzed, and whined with what sounded like hordes of wasps and hornets but were, of course, bullets. Far from being crushed, the Germans were in full possession of senses better than our own; their smartest snipers and machine-gunners were coolly waiting for us. G.H.Q., as was afterwards realised, had handed the battle to them by snobbishly distinguishing us officers from the men, giving us revolvers instead of rifles and marking our rank plainly upon our cuffs. The 'gibbering imbeciles' confronting us were thus enabled to pick off the officers first, which they had been carefully instructed to do, leaving our army almost without leadership.

Many of the officers in my battalion were struck down the moment they emerged into view. My company commander was shot through the heart before he had advanced a step. Neville, the battalion buffoon, who had a football for his men to dribble over to the 'flattened and deserted' German lines and was then going to finish off any 'gibbering imbecile' he might meet with the shock of his famous grin (he had loose dentures and could make a skull-like grimace when he smiled), was also instantly killed, and so was fat Bobby Soames, my best friend. I had spent the previous evening with him and he had said to me quietly, without emotion, 'I'm going to be killed tomorrow. I don't know how I know it but I do.' How far I myself got I don't remember; not more than a couple of hundred yards is my guess. I flew over the top like a greyhound and dashed forward through the wasps, bent double. Squeamish always about blood, mutilations and death, averting my gaze, so far as I could, from the litter of corpses left lying about whenever we marched up to the line through other regiments' battle-fields, never hurrying when word was passed down to me, as duty officer in the trenches, that someone had been killed or wounded, in the hope that, if I dawdled, the worst of the mess might be cleared up before I arrived, my special private terror was a bullet in the balls, which accounts psychologically, for it was, of course, unavailing physically, for the crouched up attitude in which I hurled myself at the enemy. The realisation that I was making an ass of myself soon dawned; looking back I saw that my platoon was still scrambling out of the trench, and had to wait until they caught up with me. My young Norfolk servant, Willimot, who then walked at my side, fell to the ground. 'I'm paralysed, sir,' he whimpered, his face paper-white, his large blue ox-like eyes terrified. A bullet, perhaps aimed at me with my revolver and badges, had severed his spine. My platoon-sergeant, Griffin, lifted him into a shell-hole and left him there. Then I felt a smack on my left upper arm. Looking down I saw a hole in the sleeve and felt the trickling of blood. Then my cap flew off. I picked it up and put it on again; there was a hole in the crown. Then there was an explosion in my side, which sent me reeling to the ground. I lay there motionless. Griffin and one of the men picked me up and put me in a deep shell-hole. Griffin then tried to unbutton my tunic to examine and perhaps dress my wound. I was not unconscious, only dazed, and I had by now a notion of what had happened. It was another instance of the credulity of the time—my company commander's contribution—that we officers had been told to carry a bottle of whisky or rum in our haversacks for the celebration of our victory after the 'walk-over'. Some missile had struck my bottle of whisky and it had exploded. Of this I became dimly aware when Sergeant Griffin moved me; I felt the crunch of broken glass in the sack beneath my arm. What precisely had occurred I did not know; besides the smarting that had now started in my arm I had a sensation of smarting in my side, so I was damaged there also, though by what or how much I could not tell. What I do remember perfectly well is resisting Griffin's attempts to examine me. I lay with my eyes closed and my wounded arm clamped firmly to my wounded side so that he could not explore beneath my tunic. I did not want to know, and I did not want *him* to know, what had happened to me. I did not feel ill, only frightened and dazed. I could easily have got up, and if I could have got up I should have got up. But I was down and down I stayed. Though my thoughts did not formulate themselves so clearly or so crudely at the time, I had a 'Blighty' one, that sort of wound that all the soldiers sighed and sang for ('Take me back to dear old Blighty'), and my platoon, in which I had taken much pride, could now look after itself.

My injuries were indeed of a shamefully trivial nature; a bullet had gone through the flesh of my upper arm, missing the bone, and a piece of shrapnel or bottle glass (I can't remember which) had lodged beneath the skin of my side above the ribs. The explosion must therefore have been fairly violent to have driven this object through my tunic and shirt. I was welcomed home like a conquering hero and was disinclined to exhibit my wounds when requested by sympathetic admirers to do so, though not disinclined to give the impression that the exploding bottle had entirely deprived me of my senses. Yet so strange are we in our inconsistencies that I was not happy in Blighty and, in a few months' time, got myself sent back to France. I was at once promoted to the rank of captain. Soon afterwards my brother joined me.

The reunion of two brothers in such circumstances might be thought a memorable occasion, yet even thirty years ago, only some sixteen years after the event, when I first attempted to sketch this history, I found I could remember of it nothing at all, nothing about my brother except—and that indistinctly—our last meeting. Doubtless my conscious mind had been dealing with it in a convenient way, for why otherwise should I remember so much more clearly the events which preceded and immediately followed it? Yet a certain measure of vagueness may be permitted, for the situation of our being together in the same regiment lasted only two months, we were in different companies, the battalion was on trench duty for part if not all of the time, my own 'F' Company was actually up in the front line, my brother's company, 'C', in which he commanded No. 11 Platoon, was in reserve. Besides being thus separated, we were doubtless much occupied with our personal commands and problems; yet I must have welcomed him when he came, introduced him to my friends and met him on other occasions—but of all that I recall nothing whatever.

My father, c. 1890

My father as a guardsman

New Brighton:
Stockley, my father, de Gallatin, Dudley Sykes

My father and Miss Burckhardt
in New Brighton in 1889

My mother in *The Merry Wives of Windsor*

My mother in the 'twenties

Myself as a preparatory schoolboy: 'Girlie'

Myself as a subaltern

In front of my trenches, some four or five hundred yards away and slightly to the left, there was a bulge or salient in the German lines known as Point 85. It was a tiresome object, for it commanded a dangerous enfilading position down the trenches of the battalion next door. In February, 1917, our brigadier decided to have it and instructed my colonel to detail a platoon to capture it. It fell upon 'C' Company in reserve to provide this platoon and my brother got the job. Did he actually volunteer for it? It is one of the many things I am not clear about, but I fancy that he did. At any rate it is the sort of thing he would have done—and the very thing he wanted. Having at last reached France, the goal of his ambitions, two years after the start of the war, he must have been longing to prove himself, and here was a situation which would have appealed to the actor in him, drama indeed, the lime-lit moment, himself in the leading role, all eyes on him. At all events, the result was that I had to make arrangements for him and his platoon to take off from my front line. Was there not a conference? The Colonel would surely have summoned us both to Battalion Headquarters for discussion and orders. I remember nothing about it. My brother's assignment was what we called a 'stunt', a common affair, in this case important if only because the Brigadier had set his heart on it. Was it for this reason that the Colonel detailed his second-in-command, Major Wightman, to supervise it and keep him and the Brigadier in touch with the course of events?

The stage was therefore fatefully set, and my brother bungled his entrance. My company headquarters was a dugout in a large, deep, straggling gully, a natural formation which afforded us, in this generally flat terrain, a ready-made covered approach to the trenches. Yet it was a notorious death-trap from artillery fire. The Germans knew all about it and its uses, for the simple reason that they had once made use of it themselves; it had formed part of their own line until they had been prised out of it; they had, in fact, built my dugout, which was therefore much safer than a British dugout, for they always delved deeper than we did. So they kept the gully constantly and accurately shelled in all its length; it had earned its name of the Boom Ravine, and there were strict orders against troops bunching, smoking, talking, or loitering in it. My brother omitted to take these precautions. He was also late in arriving. A careful timetable had been worked out to fit in with the trench-mortar fire which was to precede his assault; his departure from Regina Trench, his point of assembly, had been phoned up to us; he was ten minutes late. Unknown to him, the poor boy's watch had stopped. When, therefore, he arrived and came sauntering cheerfully down the dugout steps to salute and report, and, additional irritation, his troops could be heard chatting, coughing, grousing, and clattering their equipment in the ravine above, all the welcome he got was a rough ticking off from Major Wightman who sent him flying back upstairs to deploy and silence his men.

I remember my brother when he returned standing before me in the candlelight, bunched up in his Burberry and equipment, loaded with hand-grenades and stuck about with a revolver, wire-cutters and a Very pistol, his cap set jauntily at an angle. His visit, now that he was late, was of the briefest, it would never have been much more than to report arrival and to pick up the runner I had detailed to guide him through the darkness to my duty officer in the front line. I offered him a quick drink, I remember; he said, 'No thanks, I'll take my rum with the men.' Then, could we swop watches, his own being unreliable? He would return mine afterwards, he said. A heroic remark, and as I helped him strap on my watch, probably we both saw it unbuckled from his dead wrist. But then it was impossible to speak the most commonplace word or make the most ordinary gesture without its at once acquiring the heavy over-emphasis of melodrama. Even the tactful detachment of the Major, as I picture him, squatting on the edge of the lowest wire bunk against the wall, his chin cupped in his hand, fingering his short bristly moustache, his face averted, was overdone. Then my brother's hand thrust out to shake my own, his twisty smile, my 'Good luck', his jocular salute. 'Don't worry, sir,' said he to the Major as he left. It was his only piece of self-indulgence. His thin putteed legs retreated up the dugout steps and the sack curtain swung to behind him. I never saw him again.

The time? I don't remember. Early hours of the morning at any rate. The whole odious episode must have unrolled itself in some five or six hours between midnight and day-break. And what exactly was Major Wightman doing, planted in my dugout? It is a question that teased me thirty years ago. This was, after all, my command; all arrangements for the stunt had long ago been completed, there never had been much for me to do, chiefly to see that my sentries and those in the flanking battalions understood that they must withhold fire now and until further instructions; there was nothing left for anyone to do, except this officer who would soon be creeping over my parapet, and who, at the appointed time, taken from my own watch upon his wrist, when the Stokes guns had done their job, would whistle the signal for assault—this officer who happened to be my brother.

Was it perhaps largely for this reason that the Major had been sent up, as much to look after me in an embarrassing situation as to look after the operation, to take the whole thing completely off my hands? He was my senior officer; I would of course be under his orders, even within my own jurisdiction, if he chose to issue any. What passed between us? Not much, I fancy. He was a calm, serious, reserved man, not given to conversation, who seldom smiled. He was quite young, perhaps thirty, ten years older than myself at most, dark, smallish and powerfully built. Without exerting authority he somehow conveyed it, as he conveyed confidence. He had risen from the ranks, a man of simple education with a slightly affected note in his voice. He had the MC and a reputation for great courage and ability. One knew at a glance that he possessed both. It was difficult to imagine him ruffled or rattled; such reprimands as he bestowed were short, sharp, and cold; imperturbability, that was the note he struck. An inscrutable man.

I remember going out to watch the beginning of my brother's stunt. My thirty-year-old manuscript, of which then I was uncertain and to which now, of course, I can supply nothing new, gives me the following brief dialogue:

'I'd like to go out and watch the start.'
'Please yourself. I'd sooner you stayed here.'
'If you don't mind. I won't be long.'
'Right. But you're not to run risks. It's not your business. There's sure to be retaliation.'

Truth or fiction? It sounds plausible enough, sets a likely tone. Some interchange with this brooding man must have taken place, and I was always one of life's natural vassals, a voluntary subordinate to minds or personalities stronger than my own. My salute was famous in the battalion; no Teuton or sergeant-major ever clicked his heels more smartly, my swivelling hand vibrated at the peak of my cap ('For Christ's sake don't do that, Joe! It startles me out of my wits!' exclaimed my first company commander once when I saluted his back as he was taking a hip-bath). So the dialogue suggests me and, as I recall the Major's personality, him; on my side a diffident assertion of my own dignity and rights, together with a willing acknowledgment of his authority over me; on his, the slack grasp that accepted my recognition of its power to tighten: a dialogue which would have been very agreeable to me, I think, as I see my character now.

I have some recollection still of the place from which I watched my brother's start. It was a shattered and abandoned gun-emplacement in the ravine, which I had used for observation purposes before. It offered an extensive view of the German lines and of Point 85. My manuscript says that my orderly went with me; maybe he did, orderlies were almost permanent attachments, but I remember nothing about him; I expect that I myself, my feelings and sensations, occupied the forefront of my thought. I dimly recall scrambling up the steep earthy slope of this advanced post and lying there beneath the broken beams of its roof, my head cautiously raised above the level of the ground. Time no longer exists; how long I remained there I haven't a notion. But I recollect, as in a dream, an inferno scene suddenly opening, whistlings, shouts, rifle and machine-gun fire, advancing figures momentarily illuminated by the flash of bursting shells and the firework flares of Very lights against a background of drifting smoke, and a bunch of three or four men, curiously attitudinised, near the German trenches—then bullets struck the ground around me and one sent up a spurt of earth against my cheek. That I remember well, that little spurt of earth against my cheek. Soon afterwards shells began to whizz over and crump in the ravine behind. Retaliation had begun and I made my way back to the dugout.

Then nothing but the slow dragging of time, the racket, the flames of the candles dipping and blinking as the Boom Ravine began to boom, the occasional cascades of earth and stones that came rattling down the dugout steps from the exploding world above. The field telephone rang from time to time, the Colonel wanted news, the Brigadier was getting impatient; if the Major was resting, as he mostly was, lying on his back on a wire bunk, his hands clasped behind his head, I took the calls for him. Then—how much later?—a stumbling on the steps and one of my brother's men appeared, a smear of blood upon his face, to say he had got lost, was wounded in the hand; and the Major sitting up in bed and suddenly taking charge, his cold, cutting questions, his demand for the fellow's name and number, his orders to him to return instantly to his unit or he would have him court-martialled and shot for desertion. No soldier might fall out, said he, unless he was dead or too crippled to walk. Did I remember then my own performance on July 1 or had it not yet reached the cold, clear light of objective self-criticism?

And again the dragging of time, the candle-flames dipping and blinking, cascades of rubble down the steps, the sack curtain on the door blowing in and out with the blasts, and again a clatter upon the steps and the appearance of my brother's sergeant-major, caked in dirt, almost in tears, to report total failure, the trench-mortars had not done their job, the place was well defended, the wire largely intact, and most of the men ('The buggers, the bastards!') had got cold feet, had stayed in their shell-holes or run back, only my brother, himself and one or two others had reached the wire, and my brother had been hit, the sergeant-major had seen him fall, had seen him move, had tried to reach him, but the fire was too intense and he had made his own way back as best he could, from shell-hole to shell-hole, to report. He had rounded up most of his platoon—there had been few casualties—and reassembled it in the front trench.

Then the telephone clicking and buzzing, the signallers in their cap-comforters tapping away, the Major's calm voice reporting failure to the Colonel, more clickings and buzzings and then the Brigadier himself on the line, his furious orders to launch another attack at once, the Major's toneless stubborn resistance, retaliation was too heavy, dawn was close at hand, the Brigadier's insistence, the Major's quiet soothing voice resisting, volunteering to lead another attack himself the following night. . . . Then the Major thoughtfully sitting over the silent phone, smoking a cigarette and rubbing his bristly moustache. Then the Major retiring again to bed and turning his back upon me and the whole affair.

[67]

And my brother was lying out wounded in no man's land, and might have been the merest litter left about after a riotous party, for all the interest the Brigadier, the Colonel, or the Major evinced in his fate. And I did nothing either. Officially, of course, there was nothing to be done, casualties lay where they fell, as I had lain for some hours on July 1, and was to lie again throughout the greater part of the day in two months' time, unless they could crawl back or until it was safe enough for stretcher-bearers to reach them. If their life's blood drained out of them meanwhile that was hard luck; one did not risk other lives to seek them out and bring them in. Or one's own . . . . Officially again, the matter had nothing to do with me; such exalted persons as myself did not crawl out into no man's land to bring in the wounded, and if this particular officer had been the comparative stranger he should have been I would probably have had a nap like the Major. But he was not a stranger, and though my conscience managed in the ensuing years to blot out the details of the event, it remained for so long in my mind as an uneasiness that it must have seemed to me at the time that life was once again making upon me one of those monstrous and unfair demands with which I could not cope, that I was being put to another unwelcome test.

How long did this disgusting situation continue? It certainly worsened. My manuscript says that retaliation slackened and ceased and that a message came from my duty officer, Dyson, to say that my brother had managed to crawl back to within fifty yards of the front line and should he send out men to bring him in? It says I went out and climbed on to the roof of the dugout—a courageous act?—to look about. Dawn was breaking, the enemy lines were clearly visible. It says I returned to the dugout, where the Major was now sitting at a table writing his report, and said to him, 'I don't think it's safe to send out men to bring my brother in, do you? It's rather light,' and the brute replied, 'You have seen how light it is. Do as you think fit.' A painfully convincing piece of dialogue and not at all what I wanted. But it seems I got that in the end, for my manuscript adds that I then said, 'I think I'll go along and see Dyson myself,' and the Major replied, 'I want you here.' My answer to Dyson's message is not noted and lies beyond recall; it may have been that no one should go out to bring my brother in until further orders.

I sometimes wondered in after years about the Major, that strange enigmatic man, what he meant, what he felt, what he guessed or knew. Had he turned his back upon me on purpose, to leave me free to deal with my personal problems as I wished and in spite of his directives? It seems to me the kind of thing he might have done. And there were precedents for disobedience. Since the brothers Thorne have remained in my memory always—I can see their faces still—they may have been present in it then. Two sub-alterns, they had been in my battalion a year earlier, and the younger Thorne was one of the most beautiful boys I ever saw. He too was detailed for a raid; he too failed to return, and his brother, who adored him, went out alone to find him, in defiance of orders, and brought his dead body in slung over his shoulder, walking heavily back in the early dawn. This signal act of careless courage must have impressed the Germans, for they did not fire a shot.... But perhaps the Major found me as enigmatic as I found him, for I discovered in course of time that I too wear a defensive mask, a dead-pan look; when I think I have betrayed, under strain, the sickening anxieties and nervous fears from which I often suffer, I am praised for my coolness and self-possession, the rabbit within is not suspected. So the Major may have believed that I was exercising, in a rending situation, an admirable fortitude and restraint, courage of another kind. It would have been interesting to have had, perhaps at a post-war reunion dinner over a bottle of wine, his version of it all, but he was killed soon afterwards in the Schwaben Redoubt, a colonel then, defending an indefensible position, covering with the exhausted remnant of his command his brigade's retreat, fighting hand to hand with a bayonet against overwhelming odds, encouraging his men with his personal example to the last.

Mercifully for me this torment did not last much longer. Soon after Dyson's first message another came to say that my brother had contrived to crawl back into the trenches of his own accord, he was wounded in the leg, not seriously. And now my mind is a total blank. I have said that I never saw him again, and that may be the truth; on the other hand I remember that when I was trying to recapture this episode some sixteen years later, this particular area of darkness worried me more than any other: had not the stretcher-bearers, carrying him away, stopped in the ravine outside the dugout and called me out to see him at his request? Thought is now useless to me, I shall never know; but whether he gave me the message out of his own mouth in the Boom Ravine, or scribbled it as a hasty note in the front trench before he was carried down to field-dressing station by some other route, he certainly expressed, some-how, somewhere, his apologies and regrets, and an urgent desire to be allowed to try again, now, at once, before his leg got too stiff. He must have been bitterly disappointed to have let the side down. Whatever happened I never recovered my watch. He reported at home that I had behaved 'splendidly'.

Two months later, on April 3, I had to take *my* men over the top again, to capture the village of Cérisy (what re-mained of it) in another sector of the line, and swopped my brother's unreliable wrist-watch for that of my second-in-command, who was remaining in reserve. He lent it reluctantly; it was an engagement present from his fiancée. I promised to return it. He never saw it again either. As we marched up to the line from the billets in which we had been resting to take up our battle positions, an old officer friend of mine, Titcham—'Titchy', as we called him— waylaid me upon the route. He had joined up with me as a subaltern in the beginning and we had served in the same battalion for a year, training in England, until he managed to wangle for himself a safe and cushy job on the brigade staff. He was now a brigade major and what we contemp-tuously called a 'Brass Hat'. Seated upon his horse by the wayside he beckoned me out of the line of march. In a low confidential voice he said he supposed that, as an old cam-paigner, I had no illusions about what lay ahead, and offered me an immediate job with him on brigade staff, out of harm's way. He begged me to accept it. He had always been fond of me, I knew, indeed he had a crush on me, I think, for I was a pretty young man, and wanted to save me from a fate, of the prospects and hazards of which he doubtless knew far more than I, since brigade headquarters had planned it. 'You've done your bit already,' said he gently. But I too was a mounted officer. I had a huge mare named Sally, larger than Titchy's, the largest I had ever seen. She was neck-wise, affectionate, and docile, I was fond and proud of her, and whenever I was perched upon her back I became more arrogant and conceited than I normally was. Titchy's offer would certainly have attracted me if the bloody fool had made it earlier. But how could a company commander abandon his command on the very eve of battle? That would have been seen as plain cowardice, and cowardice should never be plain. Smiling down at him rather disdainfully from my superior mount, I thanked him and declined. I could not desert my men, I said. I then trotted after them on Sally.

A small episode from the so-called Battle of Cérisy was carried, perhaps unwarrantably, by a colony of ants, into the final edition of my Indian journal, *Hindoo Holiday*. Anyone idle enough to wish to know a little more about my part in that absurd engagement will find it there. Suffice it to say here that mine was one of the only two companies to reach our first objective, the crest of a ridge. No special merit, however, should be inferred from that statement; we only ran forward, dashing from shell-hole to shell-hole; doubtless we happened to find more shell-holes than other companies involved. Messages passed along to either side of our thin line as we lay on our ridge petered out into space; our flanks, it was soon evident, were wide open. What to do? Heaven knew. I sent a runner back to battalion headquarters with an urgent request for reinforcements and set my men to digging themselves in as they lay. While they were scratching away, like hens, with their trench tools, at the hard French soil, the Germans counter-attacked in considerable strength, firing from the hip as they advanced. The very sight of them was enough for my company. Rising as one man they deserted me and bolted. I bolted after, shouting 'Stop!'—not that I wanted them to. The vain word may well have taken on a shriller note when a bullet struck me in the bottom, splintering my pelvis, as was discovered later, and dealing me a wound where, my father had sometimes remarked, echoing Siward, no good soldier should bear one. With a flying leap that Nureyev might have envied I landed in a shell-hole which already contained one of the things I most detested, a corpse, and was soon to harbour another wounded officer named Facer, and a man bleeding to death of a stomach wound. When dusk fell upon that foolish and revolting day I was taken prisoner. Limping off into captivity, at bayonet point and parched with thirst, I picked up from the equipment of dead men bottle after bottle, hoping for a cooling drink of water; they all contained neat rum. I was reported 'Missing', with no further news for several weeks. 'I'm not much given to praying, old chap,' wrote my brother later, 'but I don't mind telling you that I often went down on my knees and prayed to God for your safety.' Some time afterwards he was returned to duty with the battalion and became increasingly fed up, poor fellow, with a war he had once thought so glamorous. It was then that he reproved me for the second time. After some eight months spent, not uncomfortably, in various prison camps in Germany, I was sent, by my father's manipulations, as an intern to Switzerland, and in the most enviable circumstances, as I now see, grumbled and sighed (the 'moan' again), as did many others, about the hardness of our lot. We were silly enough to feel guilty and frustrated at being where we were. Exasperated by my grousing letters and doubtless now unnerved by endless trench warfare, my brother wrote roughly to shut me up; I should consider myself bloody lucky, said he, to be where I was, and he only wished he were there too. On August 7, 1918, just before the end of hostilities, as he was filling his pipe in the trenches and turning round to hail a friend, a whizz-bang decapitated him. My father, I am told, was profoundly shaken by a grief he was too proud to share. Soon afterwards the stupid war ended and I was repatriated.

Eight

NOW that I am approaching my father alone I must say at once something which may not have been evident from the foregoing pages; I was fond of him and had for him a real admiration and respect. I was indeed fond of both my parents and liked my friends to meet them. My mother, who was charming, feckless, and garrulous, was an instant success with everyone; of my father, I think, visitors may have stood in respectful awe. This phrase might almost be said also to describe my own feelings towards him; I liked him, I got on well with him, but I was not quite at ease with him, nothing like as easy as I was with my own men friends, some of whom were as old as, or older than, he (G. Lowes Dickinson, Henry Festing-Jones). It would be too much to say that I was frightened of him, but I did not find it altogether comfortable to look him in the eye. He was—at any rate in this post-war period, the period where most of my memories of him belong—a kind, fond, generous and easy-going man; he was proud of me, his sole surviving son and now his heir, and, in so far as I gave him thought, I was proud of him. Yet our relationship was never to be what I think he would have wished, close and confidential, the kind of relationship I fancy he might have had with my brother. After his death, when I knew more about him and believed he may have guessed about me, I regretted this. Whether I could have achieved a nearer understanding with him must remain a question; I was only sorry, when it was too late, not to have put it more boldly to the test. It is the purpose of the rest of this memoir to explore, as briefly as possible, the reasons for our failure.

Child psychology is a tedious subject and if I advance one or two facts about my early childhood, I do so in no seriously scientific spirit or belief in their significance. I was a persistent bed-wetter. My Aunt Bunny told me that, like my brother, I was an accident and a 'little unwanted' and that some attempt was made to prevent my arrival also. Possibly it was more perfunctory, possibly that instinct for self-preservation I have mentioned preserved me; at any rate I emerged a robust and healthy child, but became a persistent bed-wetter. Psychology, I believe, has abandoned a theory it once held that bed-wetting is a kind of unconscious revenge mechanism; I am sorry if that is so, for it seems to me an amusing notion that I might have been pissing upon a world that had not accorded me the whole-hearted welcome my ego required. But whatever may be thought of that theory now, my parents could hardly have known of it then, for child psychology was not invented, nor would my father, I hope, have had the impudence to beat me for my behaviour, which he eventually did. A good deal of patience, it is true, must have been expended upon me for years, and many a good mattress did I ruin until I slept permanently upon rubber sheets. Then came a time when the practice ceased, then it began again in my early 'teens. I myself, of course, knew nothing about it, only that at first it was pleasantly warm, then unpleasantly cold, and in the resumed cycle I used to dream, I recollect, that I was standing in a urinal—a devilish dream, for what more natural than to pee? At any rate,

[76]

when I began once more to ruin the new and unprotected mattresses with which I had at last been entrusted, my father denounced it as 'sheer laziness', to which, I fancy, he had long attributed it, and taking down my trousers in front of my protesting mother he beat me upon the bare bottom with his hand.

This is not recommended treatment, I believe, for my particular weakness, or strength, whichever it was, nor is it recommended for building up a relationship of love and confidence between father and son, and I still faintly remember the embarrassment and humiliation I felt when I pulled and buttoned up the trousers he had taken down before laying me across his knees—though, memory being what it is, I can't be sure that this was on that particular occasion, for he beat me for other things as well, though not often and not hard, and if these chastisements had upon our future relations any effect, I certainly never bore him any conscious grudge.

Another disadvantage to which he may be thought to have put himself in regard to us children was that throughout our formative years he was what may be called a 'weekend' father, if as frequent as that. Having accidentally produced us all and concealed us, first in Herne Hill, where I was born, then in Herne Bay, where my sister was born two years later, he removed us again, at the turn of the century, to Bowdon in Cheshire, his own homeland, where we were accidentally discovered by his business friends. He himself was working in Covent Garden and had a flat in Marylebone where, according to Aunt Bunny, he led a gay free bachelor's life—'all the fun of the fair,' as she put it—and to which my mother was never invited.

We were therefore brought up and surrounded by women, my mother, aunt, grandmother, his sisters, old Sarah and various nurses, governesses, and maids, while he himself was an irregular weekend visitor: in 1900, for instance, eighteen months after my sister's birth, he departed with Stockley for Jamaica on a business trip. It was not until 1903, when he removed us again, this time to the first of the three houses we were to occupy in Richmond, Surrey, that he lived with us and we became a united family.

Such a father might well be an awe-inspiring figure to small children, and that was the aspect he sometimes assumed. For of course we were as naughty and disobedient as children are likely to be when reared almost entirely by sweet, kind, doting women in whom all sense of discipline is lacking. My poor, dear, scatter-brained mother to whom, in particular, we paid so little heed, would sometimes be driven by our unruliness, impertinence, or downright cruelty to say, 'I shall have to tell your father when he comes,' and occasionally, provoked beyond endurance, she did—and that was how I got my beatings. The dogs too. We always had household dogs, and my father was dispenser of justice to them also, for no one but he would 'rub their noses in it' to house-train them, or take punitive action against them, the 'good hiding', for other offences. It is fair to say that he came to us generally in the guise of Father Christmas, loaded with presents; but if we or the dogs were in disgrace he came as a figure of retribution, and it may be that, for this reason, he did not perfectly earn his way into my childish heart. But I would not care to make too much of all this as affecting the confidential relationship he himself offered my brother and me some years later.

It must have been about the year 1912, when I was turned sixteen, that he invited the two of us into the billiard-room of Grafton House, the second and largest of our three Richmond residences, for a 'jaw', which could hardly be called 'pi' and which he himself described as 'man to man'. We were both at the age when boys have normally discovered the pleasures of masturbation, and if that delightful pastime can be over-worked, no doubt we were overworking it. Probably we both looked a trifle yellow and my father thought the moment had come for a friendly chat. The precise way he approached this delicate subject I don't recall; I am sure he did it as decently as could be done in the circumstances—the circumstances being that he had left it all rather late. The ground for such intimacies needs some preparation, and in common with many English children of our class and time our education in such matters had been totally neglected. Worse than neglected, I, at least, had been misled and reached my preparatory school supposing that I had been delivered to my parents by a stork, a naivety that won me the ridicule of other boys. Indeed, considering what I afterwards learnt of my father's behaviour, and of the licence and impropriety of his relationship with my mother, I think it a trifle dishonest of them to have excluded me so completely from that freedom of thought in which they themselves seem to have indulged. At any rate, by the age of sixteen, such knowledge of sex as I had gained I had gained for myself, and it had become tinged with slyness and guilt.

My father had sent my brother and me to Rossall School, preparatory and public, in Lancashire, his own territory, partly because he believed it to be a good, healthy, roughish school where we would get plenty of exercise and have 'the corners knocked off us', partly because his own North Country friends, such as Captain Bacon, sent their boys there, partly to put us out of reach of the 'molly-coddling' influence of the women. I was a cherubic little boy with large blue starry eyes; my first nickname was 'Girlie', and at the public school older boys soon began to make advances to me. In my very first term there the head of my house, who seemed to me more like a man than a boy, used to sit on my bed in the darkness, night after night, begging to be allowed in and whispering into my ears things that terrified me almost to tears. He never got his way with me, whatever his way may have been, and for long after he left, happily for me at the end of that term, I continued to hate his memory and think of him as the devil. I don't remember when I started to masturbate, but this was my first introduction to love. Later, a ginger-headed boy used to crawl across the dormitory floor to my bed after lights out and, lying on his back on my strip of carpet, beseech me in whispers to let him in, or, failing that, to stretch down my hand. Him too I resisted for a time, but he was more my own age than my previous wooer, less alarming, and I was eventually cajoled into stretching down my hand. I remember that I found the touch of his hot flesh and the smell of his stuff on my fingers more repugnant than exciting; for a long time I disliked the smell of semen, unless it was my own; I have never been able to enjoy other people's smells—farts, feet, armpits, semen, unwashed cocks—as I enjoy mine. Later still I became more accustomed to the prevalent depravities of this excellent school, so discerningly selected by my father, in which I was never bullied or, when my first too mysterious and monstrous wooer had gone, unhappy. A shameless and amusing boy named Jude, who sat beside me in class, had opened the seams of his trouser pockets, so that his own hand or that of any willing friend could have ready access to the treasure, not hard cash but hard enough, that stood within. My left hand was sometimes guided through the open seam on to Jude's body as we sat poring over our books—though I remember wishing that it could have been the body of his younger brother instead, who was more attractive but not in my form. This led to holes being made in *my* pockets, but whether Jude's hand or anyone else's, except my own which was frequently there, was ever permitted to enter I don't recall. Indeed, when I try to think back to my schooldays, I remember only my hand, not often and always by invitation, upon a few other boys, not their hands upon me, and if this is true I can suggest a physical reason for it to which I shall come later. I see myself, then, gazing back, as an innocent, rather withdrawn, self-centred boy, more repelled by than attracted to sex, which seemed to me a furtive, guilty, soiling thing, nothing to do with those feelings I had not yet experienced but about which I was already writing a lot of dreadful sentimental verse, called romance and love.

This, then, returning to my father, was one of the young minds to which he addressed himself in the billiard-room of Grafton House in 1912. He admitted, I remember, his own early participation in the practice in which he thought it advisable to counsel moderation, then took occasion to add—getting it all off his chest in one and providing for the future as well as the present—that in the matter of sex there was nothing he had not done, no experience he had not tasted, no scrape he had not got into and out of, so that if we should ever be in want of help or advice we need never be ashamed to come to him and could always count on his understanding and sympathy. That this was an excellent and friendly speech I realised when I was older; that I never took advantage of it is the whole point of this book; even at the time, my brother thought that the 'old man' (my father was then forty-eight) had behaved 'very decently'; but I myself was embarrassed and shocked. I had never associated my father with sex, indeed it was hardly more than a couple of years ago that I had innocently failed to associate him with the production of myself. Deprived of my stork, I was brought to understand, without ever pondering it, that many years ago my parents had come together to create a family; that was all. It was what people married for and they had achieved it. Since then, of course, there had been nothing more for them to do but raise and protect us and work for our good.

To hear my father now complacently admitting to, even boasting of, extensive sexual misconduct was disconcerting and distasteful. Indeed it had absolutely no reality and I put it aside. My brother and I never discussed it, and for a great many years I did not think of it again or wonder what exactly my father had meant or what he had done. Whatever it was it lay in a remote past, and there it remained. It made no difference whatever to my present view of him, and of my mother, as staid, elderly people who, all passion spent, had fulfilled their lives in the creation of ourselves. Physical love belonged to the young. It did not enter my head even that my father might still be having congress with my mother, let alone with anyone else; all that belonged to the past; they slept now in separate bedrooms; their sexual day was done.

Nine

IF such innocence looks odd in a schoolboy of sixteen (and I don't know if it does), I shall seem odder still when I say that these somewhat inhuman views I took of my father in his middle age as a sexually abdicated man persisted almost to the day of his death, more than fifteen years later. It must be remembered, however, that our lives together were interrupted by the war, which kept me from home almost continuously for four years; when I returned after the Armistice, adult and enlightened, there were reasons for consigning him, without much thought, to the sexual shelf. One of these was health. But first of all I must describe him as I recall him best, during the 'twenties.

He was a very large man, tall and heavily built, the heaviness of his frame increasing with age. As a trooper he had been almost perfectly proportioned, I believe, according to Army standards, able to hold sixpences between his thighs, knees, calves and ankles when he stood upright with his legs close together, but the broad shoulders sagged forward more and more in late middle age until he acquired a top-heavy, unwieldy look. Upon these shoulders was set a large head, which may be called grand, with a wide, intelligent forehead, a prominent supraciliary ridge, and the strong features of an elder English statesman. My mother called him 'Punch', but that suggests an exaggeration of feature he did not possess; his nose and chin were both strong but there was nothing nut-crackery about them.

His face was fleshy and venous, becoming rather jowly; his complexion ruddy. Thin on top, his greying hair was full at the sides and back; a thick moustache adorned a pleasant mouth in which, most of the time, a Jamaican cigar was tucked. I don't remember him as a smiling man, though he was a cheerful one; he would laugh and chuckle, but his mien generally was serious and attentive; the smile, if he were pleased or amused, was conveyed more by voice, manner, and small facial movements than by any display of teeth. In one of his eyes, which were wide and blue and greatly magnified by his horn-rimmed spectacles, he had a pronounced cast.

Strangely enough, considering the condition of his own, my father held decided views, often stated, of where eyes should be placed and what they ought to do. He was liable, in the early 'twenties, to come out with a number of maxims, old adages common to his generation, perfectly absurd for the most part and out of which we managed to joke him, a process to which he was easily amenable. Among them were two 'chaps' who came in for very severe strictures: there was the 'chap who doesn't look you straight in the eyes' and there was the 'chap whose eyes are too close together': neither could be trusted. These quaint fancies, which I reported among my friends, had upon us all a somewhat self-conscious effect: should we pass muster? I have said elsewhere that I did not find it alto-gether comfortable to look my father in the eye; this was partly due to his maxim, partly to the fact that I myself don't much like looking people straight in the eyes, and partly to his cast or squint which made it difficult, in his case, to do so. The consequent tests were sometimes unnerving. His own gaze, which perhaps he supposed straight, was ever full, thoughtful and prolonged, and it was his habit, according to the distance from him one happened to be sitting, sometimes to lower his head and regard one over the rims of his spectacles, a cross-examining look, sometimes to tilt back his head for a better focus. Thus with his magnified blue eyes swimming behind the lenses, he fixed one, yet not, as it were, quite in one's place, his cast causing the beams of his lamps to intersect too soon and pull one in, so that one sometimes felt not merely scrutinised but trapped at an uncomfortable distance, at too close quarters. My own eyes, I remember, when I was younger, often felt as though they were starting from their-sockets under the strain of bravely meeting his; if my self-conscious gaze so much as wavered, I thought, the game would be up, my guilt established.

His general physical effect, then, may be described by such words as 'impressive', 'authoritative', 'commanding', but in fact, at any rate in domestic life, he exerted little authority and did not command. To what extent he directed his business I do not know; he certainly did not direct his home. Even in family quarrels, the only ones we ever had, the jealous disputes that broke out between my sister and mother, he seldom intervened, he did not take sides and put people in their places, though there were many times when he should have done so. Whatever he thought, and it was easily guessed, for the faults were easily seen, he kept to himself until, later, he might give it private expression to me in some rueful comment. I think myself that this massive and commanding appearance really sheltered a timid, unassertive, tolerant spirit, rather child-like and secretive, often obstinate, but diffident rather than self-confident, one who preferred to stand outside of life and observe it, not (as he would have phrased it) to 'put one's oar in'.

A short dialogue from one of my notebooks sets the prevailing domestic tone. My father and I are drinking an aperitif with some guests before dinner, awaiting the appearance, always late, of my mother and sister who are dressing upstairs. The butler brings in the first course, and my father says:

'What is it, Avery?'
'Fish, sir.'
'Hot or cold?'
'Hot, sir.'
'Ah well, it will be cold by the time the ladies arrive.'

It might be thought to follow from all this—and, when one remembers the end of the de Gallatin affair, it seems to me revealing—that he deeply disliked and carefully avoided being emotionally upset. It was perhaps to protect himself that he interfered so little in my sister's stormy affairs; he did not know how to cope with tempers and tears. He would not read the books or see the plays I sometimes recommended if he knew them to be at all tragic and harrowing. Once I trapped him into seeing Masefield's *Nan*, telling him it was a comedy, and he was wary of me afterwards. He went to the first night of the 300 Club's presentation of my own play *The Prisoners of War*, harrowing enough in all conscience, but would not join my party. He took a ticket all by himself at the back of the dress circle so that he could get out quickly and unseen. He had already read the play and knew what he was in for. The Palladium and the Tivoli, where he could have a good laugh and an eyeful of chorus girls, were his mark, Sexton Blake his favourite reading. To finish him up, his manners were always courteous, he was kind. He had very beautiful large hands, and the only lack of refinement I remember in him was an unconscious habit he had, while reading his newspaper in his armchair, of picking his nose abstractedly and rolling the little bit of snot between his thumb and forefinger.

The cast in my father's eye was caused by pain.* He was in pain so frequently during the 'twenties that it has become, in my recollection of him, almost a part of his personality. We knew it as neuritis; he usually referred to it as his 'jumps', 'twinges', or 'twitches'. It was not a continuous pain, I think, unless it was always with him in, so to speak, a lurking way. At any rate there were periods, days at a time, when he seemed free from it. But in the course of years it became more frequent. It might arrive at any moment and he knew when it was coming. Sometimes it was mild, sometimes it was agony. It attacked him everywhere, but its favourite seat, oddly enough considering its effect upon him when it was bad, was in the basic joints of his little fingers. It was the commonest thing to see him, every ten minutes or so when his 'jumps' were on him, suddenly grip this finger with his unaffected hand and, hanging on to it, shake all over for a moment until the spasm passed—so common indeed that in course of time we scarcely noticed it unless it was particularly

*This is conjecture. If it was not caused, it seemed often to be intensified, by pain.

bad. Then he could not hide it or stifle exclamations of pain. He might be presiding over the dinner-table in his usual genial, debonair manner when, with a 'Damn' or 'Drat the thing', he would drop his carving knife or fork and vigorously chafe the offending digit, while a profuse perspiration would break out on the brow of this huge man momentarily mastered by a pain in his little finger. I asked him once what the pain was like; he said it was as though a red-hot needle had been jabbed deep into the very bone. Yet he never complained, never spoke of his 'jumps' unless asked, and never, except for the occasional curses involuntarily wrung from him, allowed the agony he was plainly enduring to interrupt for more than a moment whatever he was saying. My notebooks give me the following conversation:

Myself (to my father who has come down to breakfast a little late): How are you?
My father: Rotten night.
Myself: Your jumps again?
My father: Yes. All night.
Myself: Where?
My father (indicating the region of the heart): Here. But it's nothing much. Only a nerve. Damned annoying though. (He moves unsteadily over to the barometer to study the day's weather.) Did I tell you that story Bilson told me the other day? There was a fellow walking down the street when he saw a pretty girl—Ah! damn you! Why can't you let up?—in a very short dress bending down to adjust her garter. So as he passed he put his hand up under her skirt between her legs. She was furious at this. 'How dare you!' she said, but he

passed on with a—Crikey!—a smile. So she called a policeman. 'Constable!' she said. 'Arrest that man! He's insulted me!' 'What's he done?' asked the policeman. She told him. 'Well,' said the policeman, 'I'm afraid the evidence isn't sufficient. You'll—Oh, drat the thing!—you'll have to come back with me to the station so that I can photograph the finger-prints.' Te-he-he. . . .

Sometimes as though ashamed of the fleshly weakness that had forced him to acknowledge pain by so much as a curse, he would pass it all off as a jest, wagging his carving knife perhaps at the offending finger in an admonitory way, as though it were a refractory child, apostrophising it with: 'Why can't you lie down, you blighter?'

It was a long time before he could be persuaded to take medical advice; it was the worsening of his condition that drove him to it. Professing a low view of doctors, whom he hurried in fast enough if anything went wrong with *us*, and the best specialists obtainable, he would have had to be practically *in extremis* before he would have summoned one to himself. However, since our own doctor, Harry Wadd, who was a personal friend, often in for a meal or a game of bridge, lived next door, he was readily available, and when my mother was worried, as the sweet, anxious lady constantly was, she would surreptitiously phone her fears to him, and soon he would come, humming and bounding up the steps in his light-footed way, ostensibly to impart to father the latest racing tip or dirty story, really to take a professional squint at him. My mother would then leave them together over the decanters and cigars. My father was sometimes vexed and grumpy with her over these subterfuges which, if he did not twig them at once, he received evidence of later when the bills came in, for Dr Wadd (despite the cigars and fine old brandy) was far too astute a businessman not to lay them on and with considerable generosity to himself. But I am sure my father was grateful to her on the whole, and her prompt action once saved his life, as I shall describe later. Eventually his jumps got so bad that he was obliged to take the alleviating drugs he had hitherto resisted ('Beastly things drugs! Can't do without them when you've once started'); these were large pink or white capsules which he floated like boats in his whisky-and-soda before or after dinner, prodding them with his forefinger until they became softened, when he gulped them down before their contents could spoil the taste of his drink. He took these in his last years whenever his jumps started, or if he felt them to be on the way, and obtained considerable relief. The capsules, I suppose, contained potassium iodide or some similar preparation, and I expect he knew that and what was really wrong with him. His jumps were 'neuritis' only by courtesy; he was suffering from a syphilis contracted in Egypt in his guardsman's days,* incompletely eradicated then and now in its tertiary stage. I myself learnt this from the doctors only after he died of it. But whatever he understood about his condition, the gravity of it must have been kept from him, for at the time when the doctors knew that he would shortly be dead he had tickets for another sort of journey in his pocket.

*I am uncertain of this. It is in my head, but I don't recall how it got there. Perhaps Dr Wadd inserted it, but I can't substantiate it. The disease may have been contracted later.

Ten

BESIDES his state of health, there was another strong reason for supposing my father's life to be as complete as it was seen: the steady regularity of its domestic rhythm—at any rate as observed by me when I was at home in the 'twenties. At the beginning of the decade he left Blenheim House, our third Richmond residence, at eight o'clock every morning for breakfast at his office. Any nosy Parker keeping a watch upon our house would have seen the front door opened punctually at that hour by the butler, and my father descend the steps in his grey Edward VII hat, his light fawn or heavy overcoat, his umbrella on his arm, a cigar in his mouth, drawing on his wash-leather gloves. He would halt for a moment in the front rose garden to exchange a word with Scott the gardener (if that bibulous old man had arrived) about the roses, the racing, or the weather, he would make some little joke (perhaps about the Epsom Salts he had just taken and would he reach his office or even the station in time?), old Scott would dissolve into wheezy laughter, the butler would stand with the gate ready open, my father would pass through and walk down Richmond Hill to the station. Punctually at six-thirty p.m. he would return for dinner, often bringing with him a present for my mother, flowers or some delicacy for the table. After dinner he liked a game of bridge and neighbours would be summoned in for it if necessary. These regular habits were, of course, interrupted from time to time; trips might have to be made to his business branches in the Midlands—Liverpool (including a visit to his old sisters), Manchester, Sheffield; if we were going to a dance or theatre he might dine us at Romano's; occasionally he would be kept late at his office and dine out alone at his club. But he seemed to prefer his home and home comforts. He was generally there for weekends and, in the early part of the decade when he was more active, might stroll on Richmond Terrace in the afternoon or take the dogs for a walk. Unless our nosy Parker had assiduously trailed him upon these walks he would soon have started to yawn.

My notebooks remind me of a special situation when, at any rate for a few years, he always dined in town; this was when my mother invited her sister, Aunt Bunny, with her second husband, Dr Hodgson Chappell Fowler, the 'Doc' as he was called, down from Pimlico to spend the evening, as she often felt obliged to do. This man, the 'Doc', was so detested by my father, who seldom displayed strong personal feelings, that he could not bear to be in the same room with him. There was nothing surprising in this; it was indeed inconceivable that anyone who met the 'Doc' could possibly desire to meet him again, the repulsiveness of his appearance and the sour, prickly aggressiveness of a personality which, since no one could praise it, was forever praising itself, were too daunting; yet share though we all did my father's distaste we managed, for my aunt's sake, to endure what we could not always avoid, and I wondered afterwards whether part of my father's quite frantic dislike of this eminently dislikable man was due to the fact that as witness to his secret marriage the 'Doc' had added to his other enormities the impudence of having a confederate claim to confidence. At any rate, the very sight of him acted upon my father like an emetic and, despite his affection for Aunt Bunny, he exacted from my mother a solemn promise that he should be forewarned whenever the 'Doc' was to appear so that he could make arrangements to dine elsewhere. This naturally created great difficulties for my poor mother, for the constant excuse 'I'm afraid Punch has been kept at his office' soon wore thin; the 'Doc', who easily bristled with suspicions of slight since it was his lifelong experience to be dodged wherever he went, smelt the customary rat, and the feelings of my aunt, who adored her disagreeable, bombastic soak of a husband and wished others to adore him too, became wounded and militant. At her wits' end (I take it from my notebook) and hoping to bring about a reconciliation, my mother 'forgot' one evening to keep her promise to my father and assured my aunt instead that he would be at home. He was peacefully smoking in his armchair in the sitting-room when he heard the 'Doc's' loud alcoholic voice hectoring my aunt as they ascended the frontdoor steps. With a single bound he sprang from his chair as though he had been stung, seized his hat in the hall, told Avery to inform my mother at once that he was dining out, left the house by the back door and returned to London.

My mother (in a fluster, entering the sitting-room to welcome the couple): I'm *so* sorry, but Punch has been kept up in town after all.

The Doc (sniffing the air): Does Avery smoke your husband's cigars?

[94]

My mother (vague and exhausted): I really don't know. Do you smoke Mr Ackerley's cigars, Avery?

The butler (an astute young man): Yes'm, of course.

The Doc (sourly gaining one end if he had lost another): Then you can give me one after dinner, if you can spare it.

With the passage of time, the deterioration in his physical condition and the gradual onset of locomotor ataxia, which affected his gait, my father's habits altered though they remained regular. He began to breakfast at home and, abandoning his walk to the station, took taxis instead. Those were the days of his taxi-driver, Mickey. Later still he gave up the train too and was driven to and from Bow Street every day in a private hire car owned by a Mr Morland, a local man we had known for years. Before turning over to cars he had been an ostler with a stable of horses on which, as children, we used to ride in Richmond Park. His monthly bill must have been terrific, and we wondered why my father did not buy a car instead, for we regarded him as a wealthy man, but when we suggested this he would say mildly that he couldn't afford it—a remark we never took seriously. On his return in Mr Morland's car, he would still bring with him the frequent little presents for my mother, exotic fruits such as mangoes or avocado pears, marrons glacés of which she was fond, whatever he knew would please her; her birthdays and their anniversaries were never forgotten but marked by something more expensive, a piece of jewellery or a bottle of 'Jicky', her favourite perfume. Journeys to the Midlands were all given up; the only large break in his

routine now was an annual month's holiday to Bad Gastein
in Austria, a famous spa where he took the cure. For his
jumps, now largely controlled by drugs, were not his only
physical trouble, his blood pressure was high, he had
developed a paunch and a liver, and the good living in
which he indulged was not the prescribed regime for
reducing any of them. He was a connoisseur of wines with
a well-stocked cellar; of claret, burgundy, and port he was
specially fond, and often when I dined with him my
opinion on some new vintage he had just laid down was
requested. 'Do you think I'm getting too fond of my
stomach?' he once asked me; a touching question from
father to son.

From my notebooks. Dr Wadd to my mother:

'Next to me at the banquet was an old man with a nose
like a glow-worm and eyeballs that throbbed like that,
and all he could say was "What's it to be, old boy?"
or "What'll we have for our faces now?" He looked
about half-an-hour in front of an apopolectic fit. So I said
to him, "Hadn't you better take a pull, old bean?"
"What?" he said, gulping down his seventh brandy.
Then I told him and he got frightened. "What ought I
to do?" he asks. "Go home to bed and take a Seidlitz
Powder," I says, "and live on nothing but hot water
for a few days." Gawd! You should have seen his face!

That's how they all go, these chaps, gorging themselves into that sort of state, coming to you with a blood
pressure of about 300, and when you've got 'em into the
safety zone again, off they buzz on the same game and
back they come. Look at old Edward the Seventh.

Bottle of champagne with his lunch, another with his dinner, all his food cooked in oil, wouldn't go anywhere unless he could get his particular brand of brandy, sitting up gorging till three in the morning—then he'd come to us, diabetic, dropsy in the feet, lungs under water to about here, kidneys like walnuts, a neck out to here, plush pockets under his eyes, and every breath like drawing a cork. That's what he was like, and we'd feed him on dog-biscuits and gruel and decarbonise him—then off he'd go again. It's the same with old Rog. You've got to take him off his wines and brandy, cut out as much meat as possible, and keep him quiet— he's got veins like gas-pipes and they get brittle. His cerebration's all right, good as mine, but if he gets an apoplectic fit, it'll be all up with him. But it's no use talking to men like that; with their livers flapping against their insteps they listen for about five minutes, and as soon as they feel the least bit better, over the top they go!'

Poor Mother! She tried, in her anxious, ineffectual way to restrain my father; port at last had to be renounced, but all attempts to wean him from his clarets failed. Once, after a fright, she begged Wadd to speak seriously to him:

Wadd: Rog, old bean, if you gave up that rotten old claret of yours I could promise you another ten years of life.
My father: Thanks. I'd sooner have the claret.

which sent Wadd into one of his squealing, leg-slapping bouts of laughter. However, the Bad Gastein treatment was certainly effective, my father would return appreciably slimmer and better in health—then start to grow a paunch and liver again. My mother never accompanied him on these journeys; she had already begun, in the mid- 'twenties, that nervous withdrawal from the hazardous outside world which was in the end to confine her to her house like a squirrel in a cage. On one of his last visits to Bad Gastein, when his gait was getting very groggy, I remember feeling sorry for my old father going off on holiday all by himself and asked him if he would like me to go with him. He seemed surprised and rather disconcerted; it was very kind of me, he said gruffly, but he could get on perfectly well alone.

In view of all this it may be thought excusable never to have considered whether this man in his late fifties might still possess virility; the fact that women and sex were often in his thought in the form of the smoking-room story, one of which I have recounted, and in other jocularities, was easily written off as a compensation, the reminiscent after-glow of a lost libido, that substitute amusement in the old for actions they are no longer able to perform. It was when I returned home after the war, at the age of twenty-two, that I was judged old and worldly enough to share in this kind of entertainment which my father and his associates enjoyed—the telling of 'yarns', as he called them. He loved these yarns and would chuckle and chortle over them like the 'naughty boy' my mother sometimes called him, spinning them out, as time went on, to interminable lengths to delay, for as long as possible, the familiar or foreseen conclusion, savouring the smutty joke with relish as he savoured his old brandy. To my young mind these yarns were seldom good and never single; one of them always reminded him or his cronies of another; they seemed to adhere together in their sexual fluid like flies in treacle, and whenever I lunched with him, Stockley and his other colleagues in his office dining-room in Bow Street, the yarn-spinning, once it had started, which it generally did the moment we sat down to table, would go on almost non-stop, each dirty story being instantly capped by an even dirtier one from someone else. At first I thought these stories perfectly disgusting, as also the terms my father habitually employed for the sexual act: to 'poke', to 'screw', to 'roger'; and his word for the male organ, 'tool'; but I got used to them at last, laughed heartily with the rest—though I felt a transparent impostor in that I never had any to contribute myself—and even egged my father on to tell the 'latest' when we were alone, I saw he enjoyed them so much. They formed the atmosphere of good-fellowship—atmosphere, I fear, was all it had—in which he and his friends lived, seemed, indeed, the only kind of non-professional social intercourse in which most of them were able to engage. 'Rog, old lad,' Dr Wadd would chirrup, dashing into the house in his smart patent-leather, suede-panelled boots, a carnation in the button-hole of his loud check suit, 'I've just heard a good 'un, had to drop in and tell you,' and drawing my father aside (if there were ladies present) he would impart in a whisper, punctuated with squirts and squeaks of mirth, the latest yarn before rushing off in his car to perform some urgent operation. I used often to wonder what could be the source of this extraordinary folklore, this large oral pornographic 'literature', these businessmen's ballads. Who invented the things? Are they still going the rounds? Some of them were quite elaborate, almost short stories: surely the strangest example of anonymous art.

All this tittering and gloating in the lavatories of sex belonged, then, in my thought to the same compensatory category as an actual London lavatory about which my father used to chuckle. This lavatory, said he, was very popular because there were mirrors in the urinals so placed that stout old gentlemen like himself were able to view and admire their own 'tools', otherwise out of sight beneath the bulge of their bellies.

Eleven

I HAD ten years in which to get to know my father, that is to say as man to man: 1919 to 1929, the year of his death, and I was at home in Richmond for only a portion of that period. Soon after my repatriation, in almost skeletal shape, for I had nearly succumbed in Switzerland to the Spanish *grippe* and was still convalescing there when the war ended, I studied with a crammer for Little-go, in which I had failed in 1914, defeated by Paley's *Evidences of Christianity.* Easements were now granted to those whose education the war had interrupted; I passed muster and went up to Cambridge in the autumn of 1919.

After four years of active service and incarceration and at the age of twenty-three I did not enjoy it much, though why I should begin my sentence like that as if I were providing reasons for discontent I don't know. Throughout my time there I lived in digs in Bridge Street; I believe I did eventually have the chance of rooms in my college, Magdalene, and did not bother to take them. Had I done so, perhaps I should have a stronger sense of having belonged to the place. As it is, I recollect very little about my Cambridge years. I felt unsettled, restless, purposeless; I wasted my time. For some reason, or no reason—how the extraordinary choice came to be made I can't recall—I took up the study of Law with the notion of becoming a barrister. My father, who already cherished the highest and proudest opinion of my mental abilities (he used to say that I could always do better than anyone else whatever I set my mind to), enthusiastically paid my dues at the Inner Temple and boasted among his friends that the future of the Woolsack was assured. In fact reading Law, dry though it was, did not entirely bore me, I was interested in the criminal side of it, and even laboured through immense tomes such as Williams on *Real Property*, Williams on *Torts*, with intelligence and was well thought of by my tutor. But my mind was only partly engaged and the confidence in myself I did not ever share with my father began to fail; I was far too slow-witted and ruminative a man, it seemed to me, to make a successful barrister, I took only half my tripos in Law, idly turning over for the rest to English Literature— a subject we can all study for ourselves in our spare time without the need for academic instruction. Throughout my school days and Army days I had written verse; I continued to do so in Cambridge and some of it found publication in one or two periodicals and in a volume called *Poems by Four Authors*; a three-act play, *The Prisoners of War*, which I had written in Switzerland and completely recast at home before I went up, was thought to be unproducible and lay in a drawer. I emerged from Cambridge therefore with an inglorious BA degree, a handful of verses, and some lifelong friends.

Vacations had been spent with my parents in Richmond, where I had a bedroom and a large pleasant study lined with books at the top of the house. When I came down in the spring of 1921, and when I was not travelling abroad, I lived there for two or three years until I started to establish myself in various parts of London. I was now set to be a writer, and my Father no doubt made an easy displacement of the Lord Chancellor for the Poet Laureate. My study was understood to be private ground where the Great Mind could meditate undisturbed. But write I could not and during this immediate post-Cambridge period that I spent at home I became more and more fretful and frustrated, more and more persecuted—though the only person who persecuted me was myself. I had every material comfort; my sister bequeathed me her car when she went off to Panama to engage herself to an American businessman whom she married in 1926; my father was giving me an allowance of £350 a year, a substantial sum in those days; he never interfered with me in any way and seldom asked questions. His feeling for me may be seen in a short letter he wrote me during my last term at Cambridge:

'My dear lad,
I asked Nancy [my sister] last night whether you were really hard up and I gathered that you were. Now I want you to drop me a line and let me know if you ever find funds running low, as all I have is at your disposal as you ought to know and there need never be reservations between us. My faith in you is as my affection for you and knows no bounds.
Your old Dad.'

No son could ever have received from his father a sweeter letter than that; how saddening it is to read it now. The very boundlessness of his faith in me contributed, as time went on, to my anxiety. For I could not write, and if he did ask questions on his return from his office in the evenings: 'Well, old boy, what have you been doing today?' I felt ashamed and evasive, for I had done nothing; if he did *not* ask questions, I was equally worried by his silence: did he think me a 'loafer'? This, as I have said, was one of his favourite words of contempt for idle, shiftless people, and although I don't now believe he ever applied it in his thoughts to me, I applied it in what I feared to be his thoughts to myself. Had I known then that he had been something of a loafer in his own youth, down at The Cell Farm and throughout his connection with the Burckhardts I daresay I should have felt better, but my knowledge of his past life at the time was of the sketchiest. As it was I lived in a constant state of restlessness and self-consciousness. Much was expected of me, nothing was accomplished. I kept desultory notebooks in which I jotted down ideas for works that never got written, I tried my hand at short stories, macabre and in the most clotted manner of Henry James, I began a verse-play about Galeazzo Maria Sforza, a fifteenth-century Milanese despot who was eventually assassinated by two young friends in the cathedral porch for his perversions and abominable cruelties. But I seemed unable to concentrate and got hopelessly stuck in everything I attempted. Trips abroad did nothing to stimulate creative thought. I went to Jamaica on one of my father's boats, travelling *en prince* with a Cambridge friend of mine; I visited France, Italy, Jugoslavia; I spent five months in India (1923–1924) as companion to a maharajah and brought back a journal of my stay; whenever I was home again my neuroses returned. I remember that when I reached our front door on my return from India and was about to insert my key in the lock, I suddenly thought, 'Oh hell! What am I doing? I could have stayed longer in India had I wished. What on earth have I come back for?'

It would be false, however, to give the impression that I was entirely miserable. I enjoyed, I am sure, a good deal of my life. But there was always, underlying everything, this fret in my mind about not knowing where I was going, not being able to get on. I felt guilty. I felt guilty when I spoke unkindly to my mother for tapping timidly upon my sacred study door as she sometimes did, though she interrupted nothing, for there was nothing to interrupt. I felt guilty at lying abed in the morning when my father went off to his office at eight, and in the evening, when he wanted his game of bridge and I was needed for a fourth, I felt trapped. I had spent a good deal of my captivity in Germany and Switzerland playing cards to pass the time and had become something of an expert; now that I was 'free' I wished never to see a card again. I often played grudgingly, therefore, or even rebelled, depriving my father of his game and afterwards feeling a cad for having done so. I did not discuss my troubles with him, I had other and intimate friends, intellectuals like myself, in whom I confided, but if he did not actually realise what was going on, that I was getting nowhere with my self-appointed tasks, he saw I was discontented and bored, as my sister also, when she was on the scene, was discontented and bored, and this saddened him I am sure, it saddened him that in spite of all the advantages he had afforded us, advantages which, in his own upbringing, he had gone without, expensive education, money, freedom, leisure, we should seem at odds with this 'wonderful old world'.

There was, in fact, an extra awkwardness in the way of my consulting him, had I ever wanted to do so; I had an uneasy feeling that he was rather hoping I would decide to join him in his business in place of my dead brother. Indeed, should I not actually offer myself, since I seemed unable to do anything else, to this important, proud concern, with its large fleet of steamers, which he had built up out of nothing, and in which the sons of his partner and colleagues were already being enrolled? He would be pleased if I did, no doubt. Yet he never, by so much as a hint, sought to influence me to such a course; the worry lay entirely in my own nervous anxiety. In fact I recall that someone else suggested such a solution while we were at table: 'Why don't you take a job with your Dad?' and he saved my face by answering off-handedly for me, 'Joe isn't interested in bananas.' The only time he ever mentioned the matter, so far as I remember, was when I joined the BBC in 1928, at the invitation of the Talks Department (my unmarketable play had by then been published and produced, and I was a 'coming' man) on a salary of £350 a year; he then said mildly, thinking only of the cash, that if I'd ever thought of entering Elders and Fyffes I would have been started off at twice that figure. However, I never seriously thought of offering myself to him; I disliked his partner, Arthur Stockley, and despised jobs. My father's way of life, the commuting life, the regular habit, the daily papers in the same morning and evening trains, the same 'cheerio' travelling acquaintances, the passing on of the latest smutty story, and the cheap satisfaction of being recognised and saluted by guards, ticket-collectors, porters and taxi-men upon the way, seemed to me contemptible, death in life. No, freedom for me! Yet, in 1928, this, so far as routine went, was the way of life I chose and imprisoned myself in for thirty years.

So although I now see that my father was not critical of me for 'loafing', had faith in me and minded not at all what I did so long as I was happy, these nervous strains and anxieties, mere figments of my own frustrated thought, and the slynesses I sometimes practised to preserve what I considered to be my personal freedom and dignity, confused and impaired my relationship with him. Concerned entirely with my own problems I gave no thought to him, except perhaps as underlining them with his tact; yet he too, I now know, had *his* problems and might have been glad to share them with a more attentive son. It may be that in temperament I belonged more to my mother than to him; as she herself once remarked, 'I know it's not a nice thing to say, but of course the *culture* comes from *my* side of the family,' and I shared with her several idiosyncrasies, physiological or psychological: I shall extend the list later. Although my father sometimes took Epsom Salts, they were precautionary, a flush for his over-taxed liver; his bowels behaved generally with exemplary regularity. My mother and I were martyrs to constipation. She took suppositories, I lived on cascaras. Like her again I was frightened of sea-sickness and always wanted to postpone Channel crossings if the trees outside our house were blowing about on the eve of my departure. Such behaviour disgusted my father, 'mere nerves' he called it, as though that solved the problem; but as a small boy, before my operation for peritonitis, I had been liable to sickness in almost any vehicle, even a carriage or a lift, and afterwards was always sick, hideously, abjectly, groaningly sick on the most moderately disturbed sea, until Mothersill and Kwell came to my rescue. Oh those troopships during the war—was

not one called *The Viper*?—where in the darkness one slip-
ped and fell in the vomit the wretched crowded soldiers
had puked up all over the deck and each other, and to which
oneself soon added!

However, if I was more my mother's son than my
father's, that is not to say that I was ever able, or inclined,
to talk about myself to her either. Indeed I evaded her more
than I evaded him, she was too garrulous and as inattentive
as myself. I don't remember having had a close heart-to-
heart conversation with her in my life, or with him. But
then there was another obstacle that blocked the way
to confidence, an obstacle more important than anything
I have so far mentioned, and to which I must now come.

Twelve

A USEFUL vantage point for observing my father and myself together is the Bois de Boulogne in the spring of 1923. My parents were in Paris with my sister, who was working as a mannequin for one of the fashion houses, and I joined them there, coming up from Ragusa, where I had been with a young artist friend. At this time I had a flat in St John's Wood.

I remember sitting with my father one afternoon in the Bois, watching the procession of people go by. If I had known and thought about him then as much as I have learnt and thought about him since his death, what an interesting conversation we might have had. For here was the city of his romantic youth, hither he had brought Louise after his desertion of de Gallatin, here he had married her and lived with her and her parents in the Boulevard de Courcelles until she died, hither he had escorted my mother thirty-one years ago. The place must have been full of memories for him, happy and sad, and if I could have that day again, I hope I should make better use of it. But although it was jolly sitting with him in the Bois, we had no interesting talk; instead we were watching a dog's large turd, just pointed out by him, which lay in the middle of the path in front of us. Which of the people passing along would be the first to tread on it? That was our curiosity, and thus, whether it was dogs' turds, or 'yarns', or other trivialities, did all our life together senselessly slip away.

[109]

To watch the world go by—this 'wonderful old world'
as he often called it—whether in the Bois, on Richmond
Terrace, or elsewhere, was one of my father's pleasurable
leisure occupations, and when our little excremental comedy had worked itself out to its messy conclusion, we re-
verted to observing the faces and dresses of the crowd
parading before us. But whereas my father was appraising
the women, commenting on those 'plump little partridges'
he found interesting, I was eyeing the young men. Venus
herself could have passed without attracting my gaze or
altering the beat of my pulse if my father had pointed her
out.

To psychologists my love-life, into which I must now
again go before continuing with my father's, may appear
somewhat unsatisfactory; in retrospect it does not look
perfectly satisfactory to me, indeed I regard it with some
astonishment. It may be said to have begun with a golliwog
and ended with an Alsatian bitch;* in between there passed
several hundred young men, mostly of the lower orders
and often clad in uniforms of one sort or another. Even
behind the golliwog I have a suspicion that another sha-
dowy figure lurks: a boot-boy. I do not firmly bring him
forward because I can't be sure that he existed, though why
should I have invented him? In Apsley House, the first of
our Richmond residences, I place him, and he is a game,
a childish game, possibly and unwittingly suggested by my
weekend and sometimes retributive father himself, for in
this game my brother, the boot-boy and I take down each
other's trousers by turn and gently beat the bare bottoms

*This animal, about whom I have written two books, has no place in this one,
yet I have dedicated it to her, for reasons which may be found in the Appendix.

that lie, warmly and willingly, across our laps. With this forgotten boot-boy I associate the word 'brown', but whether it was his face, or his bottom, or his name that was brown I don't recall.

The golliwog has more substance. He occurred during my convalescence from peritonitis. After the operation ['It has been successful,' said Mr Cuthbert Wallis, the eminent specialist, 'but I can't answer for his life.'] my father, on his early way to town, said he wanted to bring me back a present, what would I like? Expense was no matter, I could have anything in the world I desired. I said, 'A golliwog.' I was twelve years old and my father could scarcely believe his ears. He got it for me of course; but in later life he referred to it as one of the most extraordinary requests he had ever received. Of the golliwog itself I now remember nothing; possibly the shocked amazement on my father's face smeared it with guilt; afterwards I became more cautious in concealing my weaknesses, in covering up; but the unguarded moment of the golliwog, so to speak, sometimes recurred; repress him as we may, he manages to crop up.

It should not be inferred, however, from golliwogs at twelve and the nickname 'Girlie' at my preparatory school that I was in the least effeminate. That I was a pretty boy I have already said and the illustrations to this book may confirm, too pretty I fear—beauty, among the gifts of fairy godmothers, is not the one most conducive of happiness (though I remember a man at Cambridge saying to me, 'I wish to God I had your looks, I'd have any bloody girl in the world I wanted'); but I was far from girlish, physically or in my nature; there were no marks upon me as I matured from which my father could have suspected the sort of son he had sired; I did not lisp, I could throw overhand, and I could whistle. True, I disliked football and cricket and thought them dangerous recreations, but I was good at hockey (a hard, fast game Rossall played upon the sands of the seashore) and an accurate marksman (I captained the school shooting eight at Bisley for two or three years); I grew a moustache—albeit a wispier one than my father's or the Count de Gallatin's—during the war and took to a pipe: all manly accomplishments. Indeed I was far from needing, I am sorry to say, the fervent warning I received from Teddy Bacon at school. This boy was the son of that wealthy Manchester friend of my father's whose £100 cheque I was later obliged to return, and he unfortunately left Rossall at the end of my first or second term. He was charming, clever and beautiful, with a pale milky skin and black hair, and he occupied in the regard of our English master, S. P. B. Mais, the pre-eminent place in which I was to succeed him. After he had gone I noticed a photograph of him in the centre of Mais's mantelpiece and, looking at it one day when I was alone in the room, I turned it round and found, to my surprise and jealousy, written upon the back of it in Mais's hand: 'The best boy I have ever known or am ever likely to know.' Teddy was the school whore; I can't remember whether he was expelled or departed more normally; at any rate, just before he left he took me aside and begged me, whatever I did, not to go the way that he had gone. The reason for this tardy revulsion I don't recall, only the vehemence of it. My father's friendship with his father had brought us together for a time, too short a time, I liked and admired him very much and if ever *he* had sat on my bed after lights out, asking to be let in, I wonder if my life, then and later, would have been happier. Probably not; happiness of that kind, I suspect, was not a thing I was psychologically equipped to find. In any case he was in a different house. He was killed in the first few weeks of the war.

Instead of supplying his place as the school whore, my sexual life was of the dullest. Apart from the furtive fumblings I have already mentioned, I had no physical contact with anyone, not even a kiss, and remained in this virginal state until my Cambridge days more than five years later. Other boys, less attractive than Teddy, became enslaved to me, but speechlessly; I gave them no help, they left, we corresponded, they entered the war and were killed, and when I myself, in my last terms, fell in love with a boy named Snook, I could not bring myself to touch him and it remained a pure and platonic ideal. A clue to the guilty state of my ideas of love as a pure thing, an innocent thing, spoiled and soiled by sex, may be got from a poem I wrote about my feeling for Snook in my last term and published in a magazine called *The Wasp*, of which I was inventor and editor, and most of which I conceitedly wrote myself. It was a counter-blast to the official school publication, and may have been the venture upon which Captain Bacon bestowed his £100. The personal pronouns in this poem are clearer to me than they may be to others.

> He loved him for his face,
> His pretty head and fair complexion,
> His natural lissome grace,
> But trusted not his own affection.

He watched him smile, his eyes
All lighted with youth's careless laughter;
His brain rehearsed his lies
And wondered if he'd like him after.

Then love of beauty rose
Untarnished like a woodland flower,
Which never lies but grows
Caressed by sun and kissed by shower. . . .

He would not understand,
This pretty child of many graces,
So with a burning hand
He led him out to quiet places.

This erotic little poem so upset my housemaster that he
said his inclination was to beat me, but I replied that he could
not do that because the title I had given the poem was
'Millstones'. To another master, William Furness, with
whom I was pally, I confided my passion for Snook. He
said he thought it a very good thing that this was my last
term—but for reasons which would have shocked my
housemaster almost as much as the poem had done. Snook,
said Furness, was, in his opinion, a perfectly heartless little
boy and quite unworthy of me. A third pedagogic view of
me may be added. I wish I could recall this master's name.
He was a reserved, sardonic, rather attractive, unsmiling
man as I remember him, upon whom the charm of my
appearance had failed to have the disarming effect it had
upon everyone else. Bowing low to me instead of taking
my proffered hand when I went to say goodbye, he remarked, with a faint, chilly smile, 'Pride will have a fall,

Ackerley, pride will have a fall.' Rebukes such as this are
too seldom administered; I never forgot this shocking
remark and think always with respect of the now anonymous man who troubled himself to make it.

The Snook situation continued sporadically into my
Army and Cambridge life. Instinctively evading older men
who seemed to desire me, I could not approach the younger
ones whom I desired. Eluding 'Titchy' I admired the
younger Thorne at a distance. The working classes also,
of course, now took my eye. Many a handsome farm- or
tradesboy was to be found in the ranks of one's command,
and to a number of beautiful but untouchable NCOs and
privates did I allot an early sentimental or heroic death in
my nauseous verse. My personal runners and servants
were usually chosen for their looks; indeed this tendency
in war to have the prettiest soldiers about one was observ-
able in many other officers; whether they took more advantage than I dared of this close, homogenous, almost
paternal relationship I do not know. Then came capture and
imprisonment. In the hospital in Hanover, to which I was
taken with my splintered pelvis, I became enamoured of a
Russian medical orderly, a prisoner like myself, named
Lovkin; he was gentle and kind, with a broad Slav face,
but apparently without personal feelings; we had no common language, but liking to be in his arms I wanted no one
else to carry me to and from the operating theatre and to
dress my wound, which suppurated for weeks until all
the little fragments of bone had been extracted. My memory
of the rest of my imprisonment in Germany is emotionally featureless; there were two or three middle-aged
officers, among the various lagers I was sent to, with whom

I formed friendships and whose feelings I believe I aroused and frustrated, but I remember them only as shadows.

In Switzerland I was attracted to two young men. One was a captain of my own age named Carlyon. He had an artificial eye and a dog, his inseparable companions. To say that he was unapproachable does not mean that I was ever bold enough to approach him. My sentiments for him too were confided only to my notebook in many a sickly verse. Around the other, a consumptive boy who died of his complaint soon after the Armistice, I wrote my play *The Prisoners of War*, which the poor fellow, having identified himself in it, thought awfully unkind, as well he might since I accused him, in the character of Grayle, of a heartless unresponsiveness to love without, in reality, ever having made my own feelings towards him plain—if indeed I knew what my own feelings were. A passage in this play seems to me revealing as showing how little I had developed emotionally since my schooldays. The hero Captain Conrad (myself of course) is asked by one of the other characters why he is so fond of Lieutenant Grayle. He replies, 'I don't know. He's clean. Fills gaps. . . . His life's like an open book.' ('Fills gaps' I longed to eradicate when I was older and the play was already in print; I saw that Freud had got away with more than I intended.) 'But hardly worth reading!' exclaims the other. This passage echoes my conversation, four years earlier, with Furness about Snook. I was still on the same tack, purity, innocence, and innocence is untouchable ('Millstones'). Sex remained a desirable but guilty thing.

However, my knowledge of life now began to increase. I met in Switzerland a mocking and amusing fellow with whom I became very thick. He was the second forceful intellectual under whose dominance I fell. His name was Arnold Lunn, and with his energetic, derisive, iconoclastic mind and rasping demonic laugh he was both the vitality and the terror of the community. Almost the first mischievous question he shot at me was 'Are you homo or hetero?' I had never heard either term before; they were explained and there seemed only one answer. He himself, like Mais, was hetero; so far as I recall I never met a recognisable or self-confessed adult homosexual (except an ancient master at school, called 'the Nag', who was mysteriously sacked) until after the war; the Army with its male relationships was simply an extension of my public school. Lunn lent or recommended me books to read, Otto Weininger, Edward Carpenter, Plutarch, and thus and with his malicious, debunking thought opened my mind. When I was at last repatriated and my mother's frequent innuendoes about girls and the eventual arrival of 'Miss Right' exasperated me, I lectured her severely on Otto Weininger, while the poor lady lifted the wads of her hair from her shrinking ears, the better to catch, if she must, the appalling things I seemed to be saying. Of Weininger now I recollect little; that I ever got to the end of him I doubt; but I believe that his thesis is that, in respect of the male and female principles, we all have both in some degree, individually and therefore variously blended, as though we were bags of tea; if the human race, then, were sorted out and lined up in one vast single-rank parade, the hermaphrodite would stand in the centre, the 100% male and female at either end, and infinite gradations of the mixture in between. Presumably having got so far, I must have concluded my lecture by placing myself on parade in such a position as to indicate that girls were not for me; at any rate, poor Arnold Lunn became, in my mother's anxious thought, an incarnation of the devil. It did not matter; nothing much, especially of a disturbing nature, remained in her mind for long—worry was bad for the health—and anyway Lunn, like Mais, belonged for me to his time and place; transplanted into my home soil they both soon withered away.

I was now on the sexual map and proud of my place on it. I did not care for the word 'homosexual' or any label, but I stood among the men, not among the women. Girls I despised; vain, silly creatures, how could their smooth, soft, bulbous bodies compare in attraction with the muscular beauty of men? Their place was the harem, from which they should never have been released; true love, equal and understanding love, occurred only between men. I saw myself therefore in the tradition of the Classic Greeks, surrounded and supported by all the famous homosexuals of history—one soon sorted them out—and in time I became something of a publicist for the rights of that love that dare not speak its name. Unfortunately in my own private life also it seemed to have some impediment in its speech; love and sex, come together as I believed they should, failed to meet, and I got along at Cambridge no better than anywhere else. In varying degrees and at various times I was attracted to a number of other undergraduates; I had sexual contact with none of them. So far as I know, all but one were normal boys, and the normal, manly boy always drew me most. Certainly effeminacy in men repelled me almost as much as women themselves did. But although I felt that, had I tried to kiss these normal, friendly boys who came so often to my rooms, my advances would not have been rebuffed, I could not take that step. It seemed that I needed a degree of certainty so great that only unambiguous advances from the other side would have suited me; these I never got, and even had I got them I might not, for another reason,* have been able to cope. To one boy I was so attracted that I bought him an expensive pair of gold and platinum cuff-links at Asprey's which linked our engraved Christian names together. My homosexual undergraduate friend thought him a horrid little boy and I did see that he was perfectly brainless, but he had the kind of dewy prettiness I liked, the innocent look of Snook and 'Grayle'— and innocence was difficult to tamper with. Him I managed to kiss, but went no further; the distance between the mouth and the crotch seemd too great. Yet I believe that he himself wished it to be spanned, for our last meeting took place in my Richmond home to which he had been invited for a dance-party and to stay the night, and having spent a chaste one there he remarked ruefully the following morning, 'Every time one meets you, one has to start all over again.' Another boy provided a similar but plainer and therefore sadder lesson. He was a Persian and, I thought, the most ravishingly pretty boy I'd ever seen. I knew him only by sight and would trail about Cambridge after him whenever I spied him in the street, wondering how to get into conversation. Once I followed him to the station and he got into a London train. I got in too, though I had not the least intention or wish to

---

*Ejaculatio praecox. For a fuller discussion of this see Appendix.

visit London. Not daring to sit beside him I eyed him covertly across the carriage. Whenever he looked at me I looked away. At Liverpool Street he entered a taxi and I returned to Cambridge by the next available train. Some ten years later, when I was well into my sexual stride, I ran into him at Marble Arch and managed to recognise him, though the bloom and the charm had vanished, the wonderful astrakhan hair receded. More surprisingly, he recognised me. I told him of my admiration for him in Cambridge; he said with a laugh that he had been well aware of it, what a pity I had not spoken, he had always hoped I would speak, and how about returning with him to his flat now? it was just round the corner. He was no longer attractive to me, but the glamorous memory remained and I went. Our deferred pleasures were, to me, closer to pain; to him a fiasco. He smelt rather nice of some musky perfume with which he and his flat were drenched, but my apparently artless ideas of love had no place in his highly sophisticated repertoire. He disliked being kissed, and the attentions and even acrobatics he required to stimulate his jaded sex were not merely disagreeable to me but actually uncomfortable. Within limits I attempted to oblige him, but he said scathingly at last, 'The trouble with you is you're innocent.' It was a wounding word, but kinder than the right one.

It was in my Cambridge years that I began to meet and mix with other acknowledged homosexuals. The emotional feelings and desires we shared, which, at any rate in their satisfaction, made us outcasts and criminals in the sight of the impertinent English laws, naturally drove us into each other's company and the society of those who, though

not homosexual themselves, or not exclusively homosexual, were our intelligent, enlightened friends. In such
company one was able to enjoy perfect freedom of speech.
To understand and explain oneself, which I am trying to do,
is very difficult, so I don't know whether to attribute to
mere bad luck or to the inscrutable perversities of my
nature the fact that neither in Cambridge nor afterwards
did I ever meet a homosexual with whom I wanted to
set up house. The simplest answers to our dilemmas are
not always the ones we desire. Many of my friends brought
off enduring 'marriages' with men of their own class and
kind, others with men of their own kind though of a
different class, and I myself have had some short episodes
with homosexuals who came attractively in my way;
but for some reason I never established myself with any of
them. Certain, perhaps relevant, notes about my Cambridge character, as I try to discern it, may be put down.
I saw myself, in affairs of the heart, in the masculine role,
the active agent; the undergraduates who seemed to me
attractive were always younger than I. I myself was attractive, but I did not like to be thought so and pursued by
others to whom I was not attracted, as sometimes happened.
I avoided or repelled undesirable intimacies. I remember
that a middle-aged homosexual novelist, whom I had met
only twice and whose name I have now forgotten, said to
me, 'May I call you Joe?' I said, 'No.' I was not out to give
pleasure but to get it. It was particularly embarrassing when
my homosexual friends seemed to fall for me if they themselves had no physical appeal. I dodged and frustrated
them and hurt their feelings. In later life, when I tried to
improve a character which I saw to be ungenerous, I found

that, try as I did, I could not produce the smallest physical response to the passions of those who loved me and of whom indeed I was fond, though not in a physical way. Thus did I hurt their feelings again. It is easier to mend one's manners than one's psychology, and it has sometimes seemed to me that, in my case, the feelings of the heart and the desires of the flesh have lain in separate compartments.

One more neurosis, shared with my mother: I was worried about bad breath. I disliked it in others and feared I might have it myself. My mother carried always with her in her bag a supply of cachous called Red Lavender lozenges. I doubt if they still exist. Chemists sold them and they had a distinctive taste and scent, pleasant and pervasive, which I associate with her, her person and her belongings. I too used to buy these lozenges to suck before kissing, and all through my sexual life I have carried something in my pocket, peppermints, chocolate, to sweeten my breath in case it was nasty.

With the homosexual undergraduate friend to whom I have already alluded I was especially thick and had for him indeed some emotional feeling, incipient at least, which he reciprocated. We kissed. He was a few years younger than myself and is my friend still. But he was sexually experienced where I was not and was already having affairs with two men much older than either of us. Perhaps unwisely he described to me their love-making, in which fellatio played the largest part. This seemed to my innocent or puritanical mind so disgusting that for a long time I thought of his friends with utter repulsion as monsters, lower than the beasts, and wondered that their faces, when at length I met them both, should look so ordinary. This boy and I, after discussing and hesitating on the verge of physical love, which was never strong on either side, decided that it would 'spoil' our friendship.

Unable, it seemed, to reach sex through love, I started upon a long quest in pursuit of love through sex. Having put that neat sentence down I stare at it. Is it true? At some point in the journey I would certainly have so described it; how serious I was in the beginning, the early 'twenties, I no longer remember. I was to spend twenty-five years in this search, which began, it may not surprise readers to hear, in Piccadilly, at No. 11 Half Moon Street, a discreet establishment someone had told me about and where I rented a room for a weekend, twice I think, in my Cambridge history. Street prowlers and male prostitutes, not many, were my first prey; of them, strangely enough, I remember nothing at all, but I find in my notebooks the following brief entry: 'No. 11 Half Moon Street, the kind of room in which one kills oneself.'

However, if I was cheerless then, life brightened for me after I came down. I met socially more and more homosexuals and their boy friends and had an affair with a good-natured normal Richmond tradesboy who delivered groceries to my parents' house but, through some kind of physical apathy, delivered nothing material to me. By the time I reached, with my father, the dog's turd in the Bois de Boulogne I was well into my predatory stride. I had just come up from Ragusa, where I had been idling about with a lisping little artist whose girlishness had ended by sickening me; my homosexual Cambridge friend was now living in Paris and we were exploring the queer bars and Turkish baths where one was able to select

one's masseur from photographs displayed by the pro-
prietor; I was busy making assignations with a Corsican
waiter in the Café de la Paix under my parents' noses.
Later on, when my play was in production in London,
actors were added to my social list; I do not like to boast,
but Ivor Novello took me twice into his bed. Though I
can't remember my state of mind at this period, I expect
that much of all this seemed fun. It certainly afforded
pleasure and amusement, it was physically exciting, and in
England it had the additional thrill of risk. A single instance
of this mixture of fun and risk may be described. Early in
the decade I travelled up to Liverpool with my father to
visit his sisters. In the restaurant car where we were having
lunch a good-looking young waiter was instantly recognised by me as a 'queer'. While my father studied the
menu I exchanged smiles and winks with this youth.
Towards the end of the meal, when the business of serving
it was over, he passed me with a meaning look and backward glance and disappeared down the corridor. Excusing
myself to my father for a natural need I followed him.
He was waiting for me by the door of the toilet. We
entered together, quickly unbuttoned and pleasured each
other. Then I returned to finish my coffee. I had scribbled
down my address for this amusing youth, but never heard
from him again.

Yet in spite of such adventures, if anyone had asked me
what I was doing I doubt if I should have replied that I was
diverting myself. I think I should have said that I was looking
for the Ideal Friend. If I had not said that in the beginning
I would certainly have said it later. Though two or three
hundred young men were to pass through my hands in the

course of years, I did not consider myself promiscuous but monogamous, it was all a run of bad luck, and I became ever more serious over this as time went on. Perhaps as a reaction to my school, Army, and Cambridge difficulties, the anxiety, nervousness, guilt that had dogged me all along the line (though I did not think of it then as guilt, if indeed it was), I was developing theories of life to suit myself: sex was delightful and of prime importance, the distance between the mouth and the crotch must be bridged at once, clothes must come off as soon as possible, no courtship, no nonsense, no beating, so to speak, about the bush, the quickest, perhaps the only, way to get to know anyone thoroughly was to lie naked in bed with him, both were at once disarmed of all disguise and pretence, all cards were on the table and one could tell whether he was the Ideal Friend. What I meant by the Ideal Friend I doubt if I ever formulated, but now, looking back over the years, I think I can put him together in a partly negative way by listing some of his many disqualifications. He should not be effeminate, indeed preferably normal; I did not exclude education but did not want it, I could supply all that myself and in the loved one it had always seemed to get in the way; he should admit me but no one else; he should be physically attractive to me and younger than myself—the younger the better, as closer to innocence; finally he should be on the small side, lusty, circumcised, physically healthy and clean: no phimosis, halitosis, bromidrosis. It may be thought that I had set myself a task so difficult of accomplishment as almost to put success purposely beyond my reach; it may be thought too that the reason why this search was taking me out of my own class into the working class, yet still towards that innocence which in *my* class I had been unable to touch, was that guilt in sex obliged me to work it off on my social inferiors. This occurred to me only as a latter-day question and the answer may be true, I cannot tell; if asked then I would probably have said that working-class boys were more unreserved and understanding, and that friendship with them opened up interesting areas of life, hitherto unknown.

Difficult of discovery though my Ideal Friend might seem, I found him, as I thought, quite soon. He was a sailor, an able-bodied seaman, a simple, normal, inarticulate, working-class boy whom I met by introduction. I already knew some of his family. Small in stature and a lightweight boxer quite famous in the Navy, his silken-skinned, muscular, perfect body was a delight to behold, like the Ephebe of Kritios. His brown-eyed, slightly simian face, with its flattened nose and full thick lips, attracted me at once. If he smelt of anything it was the salt of the sea. He had had no sexual experience with anyone before, but wanted it and instantly welcomed it with me. In fact he satisfied all my undefined specifications and, if men could marry, I would have proposed to him. He might even, in the first delight, have accepted me, for he never manifested the slightest interest in girls (he did not marry until well into his forties), was proud of me and my friendship and excited by all it had to offer—my flat, which became his second home, my car, which I taught him to drive, and the admiration which provided him with such presents as a smart civilian suit.

This boy engrossed my heart and thought for four years, but in a way I had not foreseen he was not Ideal:

being a sailor he was too seldom available. Had he been
more available, perhaps the affair would not have lasted so
long. He was stationed in Portsmouth, free only at weekends, if then. Sometimes he went off for a long cruise on his
ship. Whenever he had leave he came to stay with me;
but because of his sporadic appearances, his conventional
background, his unsophistication, and the 'manly respect-
ability' of our relationship (the Greek view of life), all my
anxieties found their fullest play. I was not faithful to him
(not that he demanded faithfulness), he was too much
away, but concealed from him my nature and the kind of
life I led (not that he ever exhibited the least curiosity about
it). I did not want him to think me 'queer' and himself a
part of homosexuality, a term I disliked since it included
prostitutes, pansies, pouffs and queans. Though he met some
of my homosexual friends, I was always on edge in case
they talked in front of him the loose homosexual chatter
we talked among ourselves. My sailor was a sacred cow and
must be protected against all contamination.

The setting of the nuptial scene whenever he was due to
arrive was fraught with anxieties. Idle callers of a 'con-
taminating' kind, of whom I had too many, had to be
warned off or turned away from the door; my boiling incontinence had somehow to be concealed; I would have
liked instantly to undo his silks and ribbons, but the conventions by which he lived required, I supposed, the
delays of conversation, drinks, supper: sex should be
postponed to its proper respectable time, bedtime; the
Red Lavender lozenges had to be handy, a towel also,
though hidden from him, to obviate the embarrassment of
turning out naked in search of one to dry us down, and

to prevent, if possible, stains on the sheets as a speculation for my char. He liked dancing with me to the gramophone, readily accepting the female role, and often when I had ascertained that he too was in a state of erection we would strip and dance naked, so unbearably exciting that I could not for long endure the pressure of his body against mine. Our pleasures were, I suppose, fairly simple, kisses, caresses, manipulations, intercrural massage; he got his own satisfaction quite soon, though not as soon as I; whether we ever repeated these pleasures during the night (we slept in one bed) I don't recall; I doubt it; since he was an athlete, always boxing or training for it, I expect it was tacitly understood that he should conserve his strength. I am quite sure that if further turnings towards each other occurred, it was never he who turned. There seemed, indeed, always something to worry about—as there had been throughout my sexual life; and when a friend once asked me whether I ever 'lost myself' in sex, the answer had to be no.

Careful though I seemed to myself to be with my sailor, my desire for him outran prudence, he began to feel an unwelcome emotional pressure, there were failed appointments when I waited for him in vain, and I started to lose my head. Advice came from a close friend of mine:

'I'm sure that if one tries to live only for love one cannot be happy, but perhaps happiness is not your deepest need. . . . The standards which are so obvious to you are very remote to him and his class, and he was bound to relapse from them sooner or later. And by standards I mean not only conventions but methods of feeling. He can quite well be deeply attached to you and yet suddenly find the journey up too much of a fag. It is difficult for us, with our middle-class training, to realise this, but it is so. Also if you want a permanent relationship with him or anyone, you must give up the idea of ownership, and even the idea of being owned. Relationships based on ownership may be the best (I have never known or tried to know them), but I'm certain they never last. Not being you and not knowing him I can't say any more, except to beg you to write nothing to him beyond brief notes of affection until you meet again. Don't rebuke, don't argify, don't apologise. . . .'

How much of this excellent advice I took, or was constitutionally able to take, I don't remember; very little, I imagine, for later on I went so far as to rent a flat in Portsmouth for the sailor and myself in order to see more of him than I was seeing in London. There, like any possessive housewife, I catered and cooked for him while he was at work, impatiently awaiting the moment of his return. One evening he said irritably, 'What, chicken again!' It is the only speech he ever made that has stuck in my mind. The end was clearly in view, but it came, strangely and sadly enough, not through anything I put into *his* mouth, but through something I took into my own. I did to him the very thing that had so revolted me in Cambridge in the revelations of my homosexual friend's love-life. This was a thing I had never done before, reluctantly since and out of politeness if requested. It is a form of pleasure I myself have seldom enjoyed, passively or actively, preferring the kiss upon the lips, nor have I ever been good at it. Some technical skill seems required and a retraction of the teeth which, perhaps because mine are too large or unsuitably arranged, seem always to get in the way. Squeamishness with comparative strangers over dirt or even disease disturbs me, and I have noticed that those normal young men who request for themselves this form of amusement never offer it in return. It is also, in my experience, a stimulation usually desired by a somewhat exhausted sex; it may produce quicker results for them than masturbation, but they are not quick, and to be practically choked for ten minutes or so after one's own orgasm has passed is something I have never enjoyed.

I suppose I acted towards my sailor thus because his body was so beautiful and desirable that I simply wanted to eat it. It was a fatal mistake. He cut future appointments, plunging me in despair. When, at length, I saw him again I asked if I had displeased him in any way. Roughly he replied, 'You know what you did! You disgusted me!' After that he deserted me entirely for a year and a half, while I pined for him in the darkest dejection of spirit and lost much weight. Then, through the mediation of one of his brothers (a homosexual, oddly enough, and of a far more affectionate character, but unfortunately too effeminate to attract me), he wrote to apologise ('I behaved rottenly to you and you didn't deserve it') and called. He had a new gentleman friend now, I had learned from his brother, who took him for holidays to Nice and Cannes and had doubtless completed his education in matters of sex, thereby arousing his conscience over me; yet I think he would have resumed sex with me too, if only I had been able to control the emotion in my voice and the trembling of the arm I put around his shoulders. He did not want emotion, only fun. He then disappeared out of my life.

The Ideal Friend was never so nearly found again, though, as I interpret my life now, I devoted most of my leisure in the succeeding fifteen years to the search for him, picking up and discarding innumerable candidates. My restlessness at this time was such that two arresting comments made to me by friends concerned for my happiness may be quoted. Forrest Reid, sitting with me one day in Hyde Park, said, 'Do you really care about anyone?' To this searching question I do not know the answer, it goes too deep; since people and events vanish so easily from my memory it may be no. The other friend wrote, 'I seize my pen to read you a lecture on your character. . . . I think you are scared or bored by response. Here my lecture ends, for how you are to alter yourself I know not; but sometimes the comment of an outsider helps so I make it. I think love is beautiful and important—anyhow I have found it so in spite of all the pain—and it will sadden me if you fail in this particular way.' This reproach was, I suppose, much the same as the first, but I see myself in it more clearly, clearly enough to hazard an answer. I got response, doubtless because of my youth and looks, more readily than my lecturer, who went without either; I was therefore, when it came, less grateful, more 'choosy', than he would have been; I was not scared or bored by it when my own physical desires were caught and held, as they were by less than half-a-dozen chaps in my post-Cambridge life; on the other hand, response from these, the boys who took my fancy, never contented me either, or for long, there seemed always

something wrong, disappointing, frustrating. The super-
ficiality of this answer will be plainly seen by the reflective
reader; I was not reflective at the time. Another friend
of mine once told me that he was able to cut clean out of his
life and thought any emotional affair that was causing him
unhappiness. *That* I could never do; indeed I may be said
to have wallowed in the very miseries he avoided; and I
sometimes wonder, though I cannot know, whether that
remark in the letter I have just quoted, 'perhaps happiness
is not your deepest need', may not be profoundly true,
whether the hardship of it all was the very thing I wanted,
the frustrations, which often seemed to me so starveling and
wretched, my subconscious choice.

My restlessness during these fifteen years increased; I
was seldom relaxed and did little writing or reading, for
what was happening outside in the streets? what was I
missing by staying indoors? I was rarely happy in any one
place, for all the other places where I was not appeared,
in my imagination, more rewarding than the one I occupied.
The Ideal Friend was always somewhere else and might
have been found if only I had turned a different way. The
buses that passed my own bus seemed always to contain
those charming boys who were absent from mine; the
ascending escalators in the tubes fiendishly carried them
past me as I sank helplessly into hell. Unless I had some
actual business or social engagement (often maddening,
for then, when punctuality or responsibility was unavoid-
able and I was walking with my host or guest, the Ideal
Friend would be sure to appear and look deep into my
eyes as he passed) I seldom reached my destination, but was
forever darting off my buses, occupied always, it seemed,

by women or Old Age Pensioners, because on the pavements below, which I was constantly scanning, some attractive boy had been observed. Yet one of my old anxieties, now in public form, persisted: I had to feel an absolute degree of confidence. Industrious predator though I was, I was not a bold or reckless one. One of my father's yarns concerned a man who told a friend that whenever he saw an attractive girl he went straight up to her and said, 'Do you fuck?' 'My word!' said the friend. 'Don't you get an awful lot of rebuffs?' 'Of course,' was the reply; 'but I also get an awful lot of fucking.' I was not in the least like that. I did not want rebuffs or cuffs, nor did I want the police summoned. I had to feel reasonably safe and developed furtive techniques to aid me. I did not like boys to think I was pursuing them, they might turn nasty; the safest thing was the quick 'open' exchange of understanding looks or smiles. For this it was necessary to meet people face to face, a problem if the particular boy was moving in the same direction. In such a case I would hasten after him, pass him without a glance (in the hope of not being noticed), and when I had reached what I considered to be an invisible distance ahead, turn about to retrace my steps for a head-on collision. If then I got a responsive look, a smile, a backward glance, if he then stopped to stare after me or to study the goods in the nearest shop-window (the more incongruous they were the safer I felt) I judged I might act, though still with caution in case he was luring me into some violent trap. The elaborateness of this manoeuvre often lost me the boy, he had gone into a house or disappeared up some side turning behind my back—and therefore remained in my chagrined thought as the Ideal Friend.

This obsession with sex was already taking me, of course to foreign countries, France, Italy, Denmark, where civilised laws prevailed and one was not in danger of arrest and imprisonment for the colour of one's hair. Many anxieties and strains were therefore lessened abroad; at the same time—a delayed conclusion—what was the good of making friends in other countries? One wanted them in one's own, one wanted them in one's home. In any case I was condemned to my own country for eleven months in the year, for in 1928, as I have already related, I had joined the staff of the BBC and was to remain in it for thirty years. My field of sexual activities was therefore confined chiefly to London, and how, in that enormous, puritanical and joyless city, could one find the Ideal Friend? Where did one begin to look? One needed a focus, such as the popular promenades, gardens, locales, gay bars, baths, and brothels so generously provided in foreign towns. London offered only some tatty pubs in Soho and elsewhere, the haunts of queans, prostitutes, pimps, pickpockets, pansies, debauched service-men, and detectives, a few dull clubs frequented by elderly queers, and some dark and smelly urinals, which were not to my taste. To hang about Piccadilly Circus and its tube station, which I often did, was seldom rewarding, and I had not the necessary patience for long-term investigations into such perhaps fruitful foci as public swimming baths, youth hostels, YMCAs, working men's clubs, boy scout organisations, etc. In the 'thirties I found myself concentrating my attention more and more upon a particular society of young men in the metropolis which I had tapped before and which, it seemed to me, might yield, without further loss of time, what I required. His Majesty's Brigade of Guards had a long history in homosexual prostitution. Perpetually short of cash, beer, and leisure occupations, they were easily to be found of an evening in their red tunics standing about in the various pubs they frequented, over the only half-pint they could afford or some 'quids-in' mate had stood them, in Knightsbridge, Victoria, the Edgware Road and elsewhere, or hanging about Hyde Park and the Marble Arch, with nothing to do and nothing to spend, whistling therefore in vain to the passing 'prossies', whom they contemptuously called 'bags' (something into which something is put), and alert to the possibility that some kind gentleman might appear and stand them a few pints, in return for which and the subsequent traditional tip— a pound was the recognised tariff for the Foot Guards then, the Horse Guards cost rather more—they were perfectly agreeable to, indeed often eager for, a 'bit of fun'. In their availability and for other reasons they suited my book; though generally larger than I liked, they were young, they were normal, they were working-class, they were drilled to obedience; though not innocent for long, the new recruit might be found before someone else got at him; if grubby they could be bathed, and if civility and consideration, with which they did not always meet in their liaisons, were extended to them, one might gain their affection.

Evening after evening, for many years, when I was free I prowled Marble Arch, the Monkey Walk and Hyde Park Corner, or hastened from pub to pub as one unrewarding scene replaced another. Seaport towns also (sailors too were jolly and short of cash) were often combed at weekends. The taint of prostitution in these proceedings nevertheless displeased me and must, I thought, be disagreeable to the boys themselves, accept it though they did. I therefore developed mutually face-saving techniques to avoid it, such as standing drinks and giving cash at once and, without any suggestive conversation, leaving the boy free to return home with me if he wished, out of sexual desire or gratitude, for he was pretty sure to know what I was after. This, I suppose, was akin to my father's technique of bribery in advance for special restaurant service, for of course I too hoped for responsiveness to generosity and was annoyed if I did not get it. A similar but more self-restrained and hazardous form of procedure was to treat the soldier, if he was particularly attractive, to a pleasant evening's entertainment—cinema, supper—give him a present at the end of it when he had to return to barracks, and leave it to him to ask, 'When can I see you again?' Thus, by implying that it was more his society then his body that interested me, did I hope to distinguish myself from the other 'twanks' (as guardsmen called people like myself) and gain his respect. If he did not turn up to his future appointment I was upset and would loiter about his barracks for days. These methods had another advantage: they disarmed, or could be hoped to disarm, any tendency the guardsman might have to robbery or violence. Such incidents were not frequent but they occurred, sometimes brutal (the homosexual who was found murdered, his penis severed and stuck into his own mouth), sometimes jolly (the Hammersmith quean, who, robbed by a guardsman of his fur coat, flew out in a rage and found a policeman, who quickly recovered the conspicuous garment and went

to bed with the grateful owner himself). Cautious and
nervous as I was, I myself did not get through without a few
episodes of extortion and theft, in France of actual violence,
so repugnant to my mind that I noticed in course of time
that the boys I picked up were almost always mild and
characterless, as perhaps they had been from the very
beginning; character tended to be difficult, and it was as
though some instinct for safety within me recognised and
selected boys with no character whatever.

As I have said, I never came so close to finding the Ideal
Friend again but, my standards declining, I found a number
of decent boys who attracted me, of whom I grew fond as
they grew fond of me, who entered my family life as I
entered theirs, and who afforded me further rests upon the
way. For one reason or another they were all imperfect,
a common inperfection being that, though obliging, they
were, like the Richmond tradesboy of my early days,
physically unresponsive to homosexual love. One of them
was married, the others had girls somewhere in the background. This was one of the first things I had to give way on,
because it was recurrent. The girl friend was a situation all
too liable to be found in the lives of normal boys, and my
formula (as I now see it) had to be modified to meet it.
Since women could not be excluded they had to be admitted; I never suffered much from jealousy and the Ideal
Friend could have a girl or a wife if he wished, so long as
she did not interfere with me. No wife ever failed to interfere with me.

These boys remained my friends for some years, until the
second war killed them or they disappeared into marriage.
They were what homosexuals call 'steadies', that is to say

they propped up one's mind, one could call upon their company and comfort if available, if required—and if nothing more hopeful offered. For valuable though they were, the belief remained that one could do better, better, better, and so one continued to hurl oneself into the fray. This *ignis fatuus* caused me to behave inconsiderately to them at times, even to hurt the feelings my genuine affection for them had aroused, and one at least had the spirit to reprove me when I fobbed him off from an appointment with a present of money because some more promising new candidate had since appeared upon the scene. Another of them, to whom in the beginning I had given bad marks, became in the end, I suddenly perceived, the best and most understanding friend I had ever made; a Welsh boy, gentle, kind, cheerful, undemanding, self-effacing, always helpful, always happy to return to me in spite of neglect, and in control (a rare thing) of his jealous wife, I realised his value so deeply at last that he involved my heart. His feet smelt, poor boy, some glandular trouble, and out of politeness he preferred not to take off his boots. He was killed in the war. When I had lost him and remembered the course of our friendship, how it had gradually sprouted and burgeoned out of such, for me, unpropitious soil, I wondered how many other decent boys I had carelessly rejected in pursuit of my *ignis fatuus*. Some, I recalled, had made so little impression upon me at our one and only congress that, seeing them again some months later sunning themselves on the grass of Hyde Park, I could not even remember what had passed between us.

As has already been indicated I was far from being the only person engaged in these activities; there was indeed

considerable competition and as time passed I got to recognise some of my rivals well by sight. Standing at the various
bars, with our token half-pints before us, waiting for the
soldiers and sailors to appear, we would eye each other
surreptitiously, perhaps registering the fact that, with so
many eagles about, if any Ganymede did arrive we would
have to work fast. A number of my own intellectual
friends shared this taste of mine and might pop in; but it was
tacitly understood that this was not a social gathering, like
a cocktail party, but a serious occasion needing undistracted
concentration, like stalking or chess. To speak to each other
would have been a breach of etiquette; a nod or a wink
might pass, then to the business in hand. Perhaps one would
meet them again later, in some other pub, beating, like
oneself, all the known coverts for the blue-jacketed or
red-breasted game. . . . And as the years rolled by I saw
these competitors of mine growing older and older,
greyer and greyer and, catching sight of myself in the
mirrors of saloon or public bars, would perceive that the
same thing was happening to me, that I was becoming
what guardsmen called an 'old pouff', an 'old twank',
and that my chance of finding the Ideal Friend was, like
my hair, thinning and receding. Most of my prejudices
had now fallen by the way, nothing in the human scene any
longer disgusted me (how heart-rending the cry of the
pervert to his sexologist: 'I want people to shit on my face,
but even when I find them they are *never* my type'),
dirt and disease worried me no more (though the state of
my breath continued to do so for ever), I kept a stock of
Blue Ointment handy for the elimination of crabs, and
weathered a dose of anal clap without much fuss (anal, yes;

I *assured* the young Grenadier that I was quite impenetrable, but he begged so hard to be allowed at any rate to try). I wanted nothing now but (the sad little wish) someone to love me. My last long emotional affair, in the torments and frustrations of which I wallowed for years, was with a deserter, who became frontally infected by a prostitute with the disease I have just mentioned. Confessing this to me when I was hoping to go to bed with him, he unbuttoned his flies to exhibit the proof, squeezing out the pus for my enlightenment. Twenty years earlier, I reflected, such a performance would have dished him for me for ever; now I saw it as one of the highest compliments I had ever been paid.

This account of my love life has taken me rather beyond my plan, but not much. I have continued it until long after my father's death, but it has a relevance to my business with him which will be evident in due course. Curiosity about myself has carried me somewhat further than I meant to go,* and to small result; however honestly we may wish to examine ourselves we can do no more than scratch the surface. The golliwog that lies within and bobs up to dishonour us in our unguarded moments is too clever to be caught when we want him—unless by others, to whom this superficial sketch of myself may be of value when I lie under another sort of sod.

---

*A note in the Appendix carries it still further and beyond the confines of this memoir.

Thirteen

How much about my nature and behaviour did my father perceive or guess? It was a question that interested me only after his death when I could obtain no answer. He was a shrewd man and there must have been clues in plenty. Though I had a few women friends, usually married or lesbian, girls in my life were conspicuous for their absence. There had, it is true, been one in the early 'twenties with whom I was very thick; it was on her account that my mother, with her innuendoes and insinuations, earned her lecture on Otto Weininger, which should have been clue enough. An intellectual literary girl, met with during a short sojourn in Charlotte Street, an artists' colony in those days, where I was to be seen about in my carabiniero's black cloak, she became one of my constant companions and a frequent visitor to my Richmond home. She was far from being a pin-up girl and although my parents, in their thoughts, may have made the best of her as a prospective daughter-in-law, I am sure that neither of them was deeply disappointed when our friendship came to an abrupt end. I had not concealed from her my active homosexual pre-dilections, which she seemed to accept easily enough at first; but as time passed she became increasingly carping and bitter about them: 'Poor old Joe! You and your boys!' One evening she said, 'I suppose it would disgust you to go to bed with me?' I said, 'Yes.' A heroic conversation in its way, for we both uttered unflinching truths, though the

[141]

heroism was more on her side than mine, for whereas she must have considered her question and the risk of it, I did not consider my reply at all, it was shocked out of me.

With her broad, heelless shoes, thick stockings, and rather scurfy, unwashed appearance, she belonged, I fancy, in my father's ideas, more to the category of 'rum ducks' than to that of 'plump little partridges'; rummer ducks than she were to be introduced by me into his house, literary, theatrical, musical and other folk, bachelors all. A constant visitor was a retired air-commodore, L. E. O. Charlton, with a charming young male companion, not quite of the same class, to whom he sometimes referred as his secretary, though one might have wondered why he should need one; there were also a young actor, who rendered my father momentarily speechless at dinner one evening by asking him, 'Which do you think is my best profile, Mr Ackerley'—turning his head from side to side— 'this, or this?'; a brilliant talkative Irishman, of encyclo-paedic knowledge, with a thin, carefully curled, cylindrical fringe of a moustache and black paint round the lower lids of his eyes, which looked like mascara but was said to be an ointment for conjunctivitis, who arrived in a leather jacket with a leopard-skin collar and pointed purple suede shoes, and lectured my astonished father on the problem of the uneconomic banana skin; and an intellectual policeman. 'Interesting chap,' said my father afterwards, adding, 'It's the first time I've ever entertained a policeman at my table.'

Even before this I must have given him food for thought. There was a very early episode, the details of which have vanished from my mind; it concerned a boy I picked up in Shaftesbury Avenue and asked my father to help. The boy was good-looking and well-spoken, in poor health and out of work. Whether I went to bed with him I don't recall; doubtless something took place between us. My father consented to see him, liked him, gave him a job in one of his branches, and regretted it afterwards, I don't remember why. I fancy the boy turned out to be consumptive, he may have been idle or dishonest too; at any rate he gave my father trouble and had to be got rid of at last. A little later I tried the same thing on with the Corsican waiter of the Café de la Paix, whom I have mentioned. Soon after our return from Paris and the dog's turd, our butler gave notice, another had to be found and I suggested to my father, nervously through my mother, that this waiter might be given the job. He was a most attractive boy, we had all been affected by his charm and friendliness and made a point of reserving his table at the Café whenever we lunched or dined there; he had taken to us and it was known that he wanted to come to England to learn the language. It was not known, however, that on one of his afternoons off, I had taken him to a *louche* hotel where I had booked a bedroom: we had been corresponding since. But my father was highly vexed by the suggestion that he should be brought over to be our butler. 'Certainly not!' he said, and added, 'Joe and his waiter friends!'

As well as 'waiter friends' and 'rum ducks', there were my writings. *The Prisoners of War* was published and performed in his lifetime, as I have said; *Hindoo Holiday* he read in typescript not long before he died. In neither of these works do 'plump little partridges' abound, the emotional feeling is all between men and boys. Indeed, poor Mme Louis, in the play, gets a flea in her ear which is

gratefully remembered even today by elderly homosexuals. *Mme Louis:* 'You see, Captain Conrad, I hear you
do not greatly care for the fair sex.' *Conrad:* 'The fair sex?
Which sex is that?' My recollection is that, although all
my friends had read this play before its publication, my
father had to ask if he might see it. Perhaps I was a little self-
conscious, so far as he was concerned, about its homosexuality; perhaps I simply hadn't thought to include him.
I gave it to him of course. When he had finished reading
it he silently handed it back, and I had to request an opinion
I felt I should not otherwise get. I expect he was shy and
diffident, for the opinion, when it came, pleased me very
much. Taking his cigar from his mouth in his rather de-
liberate way and carefully depositing the ash, he said,
'Anyone should be proud to have written it.' I did not put
him to the humiliation of asking permission to read
Hindoo Holiday, but I was cautious enough, before handing
it to him, to remove the conversation with Narayan in
which the Maharajah's sexual behaviour is made plain.
Even so he smelt a rat, as I shall relate in a moment. All I am
wanting to say here is that whatever sexual guilt I had to
cope with in my subconscious mind I had none in my
intellect; I thought, wrote, and spoke the love of man for
man and, among my friends, even among some intelligent
normal ones, made no bones about my activities. I have a
letter from Lytton Strachey, whom I knew only slightly,
which ends:

> 'With best regards to
> The Army
> The Navy
> and The Police Force'

In short, I think I can say for myself that I was generally regarded as an open, truthful man, not secretive as my father turned out to be, and if ever he had evinced any curiosity about my private life I believe I would have told him, so long as he had questioned me in an intelligent way. But he never did, though a few opportunities occurred. He muffed one of them, I another. The former came some six months after my return from India, in 1924. On the boat out I had made friends with an Italian sailor of the lower deck, who slept two nights with me in my Bombay hotel before I went up country. We corresponded and agreed to meet again, in Turin where he lived, when opportunity presented itself. It came, as I saw it, awkwardly. I had, in fact, only just returned from Milan, where I had been seeking 'on the spot' inspiration for my play about Sforza, when the summons to Turin came. This was in my most self-conscious period when I could write nothing and felt I was becoming a loafer in my father's eyes. It may be, too, though I find the episode hard to recollect, that fresh human interests had brewed meanwhile in England. At any rate I vacillated, I didn't want to go. This indeed was the very moment when that corrective friend of mine sent in his reproving shaft: 'You are scared or bored by response.' More, possibly, because I was susceptible to criticism than because I wanted to go, I went. But since I was nervous about my situation with my father I persuaded this critical friend to conspire with me in a thumping lie. I was not going to Turin but to stay with him in his Weybridge home. Reluctantly he permitted this deception. Three or four days after I reached Turin (of which visit I remember nothing whatever) my father had a heart attack at table.

Dr Wadd, summoned by my mother—the occasion when her prompt action saved my father's life—dashed in with a hypodermic syringe of digitalis and jabbed it so hastily, though successfully, into the back of one of his hands that it raised a large lump which he kept to the end of his days. My mother wired to me in Weybridge: my friend there was not on the 'phone. Realising that the game was up, he came over to Richmond and told her the truth. It was decided to keep it from my father and a wire was sent to me in Turin. I never got it, for I was already on my way home; I had suddenly recollected that my birthday was about to fall and foresaw muddlement between Richmond and Weybridge. I did not know of my father's illness, therefore, until I reached the house. Unfortunately there was something else I did not know; serious flooding had occurred in the Thames valley. I found my father recovering but still bed-ridden; he asked me at once whether the floods had held me up. I looked perfectly blank. Somehow we got round this for the moment, but I saw I had given myself away. I was upset about him, grieved to see him ill, remorseful for having lied to him. A day or two later, when he was better able to talk, I went to him and said, 'I've got something to tell you, Dad. I lied to you about Weybridge. I didn't go there at all.' He said, 'I know, old boy. I knew you were lying directly I asked you about the floods.' I said, 'I went to Turin.' 'Turin, eh?' he said. 'That's rather farther,' and then, 'I'm very sorry to have mucked up your plans.' This was sickening. I said, 'I'm very sorry to have lied to you. I wouldn't have done so if you hadn't once said something about me and my waiter friends. But I don't really mind telling you. I went to meet a sailor friend. . . .' But he interrupted me with 'It's all right, old boy. I prefer not to know. So long as you enjoyed yourself, that's the main thing.' Thus did he close the door in my face. At that moment, perhaps through some guilty need to confess, I would, for better or for worse, have told him anything in the world.

The second opportunity occurred a couple of years later when he was reading the typescript of *Hindoo Holiday*. We were alone in the dining-room when he looked up at me and asked, 'Was the Maharajah a bugger?' I wish I had said yes. I wonder how the conversation would have continued, if at all, from there. And I dislike lying, though I have got used to it now in the course of years. But he had chosen an unfortunate, for him typical, word. I was romantic about homosexuality then, 'bugger' was a coarse, rude, objectionable word I did not care for and never used, except as a joke. I could not allow it to be applied to myself or my friends. I said no, and closed the door on him.

There was to be a final eleventh-hour chance, but we never took it. My father's dying began with an illness quite different from the one that finished him off. At dinner one evening, when Dr Wadd was present, he poked out his tongue at him and said, 'What do I do about that?' There was a large, thick, purplish patch in the middle of it. He must have had it secretly in his mouth for some time and known what it was. 'That's all right, Rog, old boy, a spot of radium will soon clear it up.' For some weeks he lay in Wadd's hydro next door with radium needles in his tongue, very patient, but getting more and more vexed with his old friend Wadd (whom he had long seen through as a humbug) who, believing him to be wealthy and knowing

[147]

him to be dying, was now fleecing him in every possible
way. Specialists visiting other patients would be winked in
to take a squint at him, would amuse him with a 'yarn'
(which my father was now unable to cap, since he could not
speak), and then send in a bill for ten guineas. These bills
my father never disputed, grumble about them though
he did, but he was glad to get out of Wadd's clutches.
Very groggy on his legs he went down to a hotel in Southsea to recuperate from his cancer, which had left him with a
sore tongue, and to die of other things. But he was not to
escape medical vulturism, for he carried with him a letter
from Wadd to the Southsea doctor appointed to attend
him, which somehow I saw. The part that I remember
said that he could afford good fees. Soon after he was
installed I visited him and found him in his bedroom
washing out his mouth with permanganate of potash.
He said, 'You know, it's a funny thing but my old dad had
cancer of the tongue and I thought him an old man. In fact
he was about the same age as I am. And now *I* have cancer
of the tongue and I don't feel old at all.' I too thought my
father an old man; he was the same age as I am as I write
this book and, although I have not yet had cancer of the
tongue, I don't feel old either.

Not long after this he had the first of a series of strokes,
expected by the doctors. Syphilis had begun its attack upon
the blood vessels of the brain. The stroke was slight and he
was able to get about after it with the aid of sticks. He
remarked to me then with a chuckle that the thing that had
worried him most was that he might not be able to 'get
the horn' again, but thank heaven the doctor had reassured
him on that point.

It was at this time (the year was 1929) that I was conducting my affair with my English sailor who, as I have said, was stationed in Portsmouth, which is contiguous with Southsea. I forget if I had already established us both in the Portsmouth flat; at any rate I was constantly driving down from London to see him. Now that my father had chosen Southsea for his convalescence (was it because he knew I went there so often?) I wanted to visit him too; but the sailor had the larger share of my interest and, not wishing to miss any opportunity of seeing him, the most convenient arrangement seemed to be to bring them together. This worked very well; my father was charming to this inarticulate, monkey-like boy who could not express himself without the help of manual gesture, of whom he could not have made much, for there was not much to make. He must surely have wondered—if he had not guessed—what his son, whose photo had lately appeared in *Vogue* under the caption 'We Nominate for the Hall of Fame', after the London production of *The Prisoners of War*, could possibly see in so dumb a companion; yet he accepted him with grace and good humour, invited him two or three times to dine with us both in his grand hotel, joked with him and teased him to make him laugh, and took an interest in his pursuits, his naval life, his boxing, and his deep-sea diving. Thinking back at it all now, I expect he must have been pretty bored with this boy, and I wonder whether, by having him with me so much, I may not have forfeited my last chance of a private conversation and understanding with my father. I doubt it. The sailor, it should be said, was helpful and attentive to him too, so far as, in such daunting surroundings, his natural diffidence allowed him to exert himself; he helped him out of his chair and supported him along the corridors; when my father was feeling equal to it we drove him about in my car. But if there were opportunities for a quiet conversation with me he did not take or make them; he asked no questions, invited no confidence—and offered none; if I had my secret life, he had his.

One evening he remarked to us jovially at table that he was particularly pleased with himself, he had lately had a wet dream, a thing that had not happened to him for months. None of these merry remarks of his had, for me, the least significance; I took them all as the rather wistful jollities of the sexually abdicated. When we were escorting him to his bedroom afterwards, the lift-man said to him, 'The lady from the Pier Hotel has phoned, sir. She wants her suitcase back at once.' A momentary silence ensued; then my father said rather gruffly, 'Come in and get it. You'll find it under the bed.' The sailor and I covered up this awkward indiscretion as best we could with small-talk; we speculated about it when we left. A similar indiscretion occurred a little later, this time by way of the telephone operator, and the name of the lady at the Pier Hotel, who wished to speak to him, was supplied. It was Muriel. My mother and sister happened to be having tea with him; he said briefly, by way of explanation, 'You remember I've spoken about her. An old friend.' My mother, who was the vaguest of creatures, made nothing of this, but it gave my sister food for thought. In fact my father had mentioned this lady to us, but not often and not for many years; she had been actively engaged, we dimly recalled, in some ambulance or hospital service, of patriotic interest to him, during the war, and he had

occasionally alluded to her in laudatory terms as a splendid
woman who had done wonderful work for the sick and
wounded in various countries and received for it sundry
foreign decorations. But 'old friend' of his though she
might be, he had never brought her to our house and, so
far as I could recollect, none of us had ever met her. Now,
it appeared, she had graciously emerged from her ambulance to look after him in his illness, for which we felt
extremely grateful to her. My mother could not have
coped with sickness at such a distance, it plunged her into a
state of agitation even at home, and any patient nursed by
her would soon have been driven round the bend. Nervous
of life, frightened of death, surrounded by sedatives and
boxes of glycerine suppositories, she was already forming
that eccentricity of habit which was soon to confine her,
an affable chatterbox and for a time a secret drinker, with
a female help and a succession of Sealyham dogs, within
the sheltering walls of her own dwellings for another seventeen years. Not without reluctance did she allow herself
to be driven to Southsea by my sister to visit my father;
when his condition worsened she went no more until his
death; she excused herself from going up to see him dead
(my notebook contains the entry 'Mother and Head-
waiter' but alas I can't remember what it means, something
characteristic and bizarre, no doubt) and did not attend
his funeral in Richmond. I saw that the very thought of it
upset her and advised her to stay at home.

Now that the presence and name of the lady at the Pier
Hotel were out, I daresay my father relaxed whatever
caution he had ever employed, at any rate so far as I was
concerned, and started to let slide what he saw he could no

longer prop up, for I began to collide with her and was introduced. She was a tall, rather coarse-looking woman to whom I did not take, but she was clearly fond of him and addressed him as 'Dear' and 'Dearest'. She described herself as a widow with three daughters, and she had known my father for twenty years. A little later, when I called with my sailor, I found her with the youngest of her daughters, a girl of seventeen, who called my father 'Uncle' and 'Darling' and bore so marked a resemblance to him and my sister that I was not wholly unprepared for the revelations that followed his death, which occurred soon afterwards.

The last time I saw him alive another stroke had left him partially paralysed. He was conscious but did not know if he was on his back or his side and was under the delusion that he was too near the edge of the bed and might fall out. He wanted to pee, he said, and asked me to fetch his bed-bottle, but it was a great struggle for him to get into the right position to insert his 'tool' into it. I helped him, rolling him with difficulty on to his side, and tried to guide him into the bottle. I had handled a good many 'tools' in my life, but with this dread gun that had shot me into the world I may have been awkward and clumsy; at any rate he pushed my hand away and finished the job himself. Only a few drops came out. Even in this extreme moment he said no more to me, except, dismissively, that there was nothing more that I could do. To Muriel afterwards he said with a groan, 'I wish I could die'; he would never have said so meek a thing to me.

News that he was sinking reached me at the BBC; by the time I got to Southsea he was dead. Muriel met me and took me up to his darkened room; she had already prepared him.

I stood just within the door looking across the twilit room at the large, still figure upon the bed. He had been laid out under a sheet, his hands folded on his chest, his head with its calm, majestic, now waxen and remote face propped against pillows. Death has always filled me with awe and, perhaps inherited from my mother, repugnance. Now I wanted only to get away. I had done what was expected of me, I had seen my dead father; I wanted to go. But Muriel, whom I had forgotten, was in the shadows observing me, with understanding and contempt. 'What are you standing there for?' she suddenly exclaimed. 'Are you afraid of the dear old chap? What is there to be frightened of? Come along and give him a kiss, the darling old boy.' And repeating 'Dear old boy', 'Darling old Rog', she stood beside the bed patting and kissing his dead face and trying to pinch up his cheek in a playful, affectionate, proprietory way, but the flesh was stiff and would not come up in her fingers. She had placed between his folded hands a small sprig of heather and—it was good of her, I realised later— a snapshot of my brother, sister and myself taken as children.

Like so many other things that might be expected to have made upon me an indelible impression, the remainder of that day has been expunged from my memory. Did she trouble to explain herself to me then? My fancy is that she was brusque and hostile, said that she did not suppose she would see much more of me and that she had already taken from my father's personal possessions such money and objects as he had promised her, including the tickets for Bad Gastein where he had planned to take her had he recovered.

Fourteen

THE full tale of my father's deception was made known to me in two letters, sealed in a single envelope addressed to me and marked 'Only in the case of my death', which I found in his office. The letters were separated in time by seven years; the first was dated October 21, 1920, the second December 13, 1927. I will give them in full.

'[1920] My dear lad,
Seeing you this morning a grown man, with every sign of a great intelligence and a kindly nature towards human frailties, I think I ought to leave you a line to explain one or two things in my past which it is inevitable you will have to consider in case anything happens to me in the near future. I shan't leave much money behind me, not being built that way, but I don't think there will be any debts worth mentioning. Since I came to man's estate I have provided for my sisters and I wish them to have one thousand pounds clear. My will leaves everything to Mother, but you can arrange things for me in these matters I write of, as since I made my will I have arranged an agreement with Elders and Fyffes that in case of my death during the next ten years she will get £1500 a year for the remainder of that period. If I *don't* die she ought to be all right. Now for the 'secret orchard' part of my story. For many years I had a mistress and she presented me with twin girls ten years ago and

another girl eight years ago. The children are alive and are very sweet things and very dear to me. They know me only as Uncle Bodger, but I want them to have the proceeds of my Life Insurance of £2000 (fully paid up and now worth £2500) in the Caledonian Insurance Coy; the policy being with any private papers in the safe here. I would also like £500 paid to their mother. She still keeps her maiden name and doesn't live with the children. You will now begin to realise why I didn't keep a car!! I am not going to make any excuses, old man. I have done my duty towards everybody as far as my nature would allow and I hope people generally will be kind to my memory. All my men pals know of my second family and of their mother, so you won't find it difficult to get on their track.

Your old Dad.'

'[1927] Dear lad,
I opened the envelope enclosing this other document just now to refresh my mind. Seven years have passed since I wrote it and seven years of expensive education for the three girls etc. etc. It means that my estate has dwindled almost to vanishing point and my latest effort viz. buying a house in Castelnau for them has about put finishing touches. The position today is: Two policies of £500 each, Harry Wadd owes me £514, and my fully paid policy worth £2765 in pawn with my bank against an overdraft. Mother is entitled to draw about £3000 a year if I die before 1930 and after that probably E. & F. will carry on a pension for her in reward for my long service. At any rate I hope so. Muriel *must* have the

£2000 policy. I have always promised her that and she certainly has loved me for all these years and when you see her and her decorations for work done during the war, OBE, Italian Victoria Cross etc. etc. and you see the girls and hear of their love for me, you will see that all that can be done is done for her. You met her lunching with me last year, and you and Nancy met the children years ago at the Trocadero with old Miss Coutts.

Your old Dad.'

My father died in October 1929, and my part in the transactions that followed has long filled me with various irritations ranging from doubt to disgust. We had never been brought up to think of money, it was always there and as much as we wanted, and if it occurred to me at all that my mother's share of these lean leavings looked somewhat thin (for how much would she get, in October 1929, out of the ' £3000 a year if I die before 1930' ?), the thought did not affect what I considered my bounden duty, indeed my instant consent, to the old chap's wishes. They must be honoured, of course, and the office would naturally provide for my mother. In this frame of mind, as innocent as his own, I went to see his 'men pals', not one of whom, after a lifetime of friendship, had been to visit him in his last illness, but whose only manifest concern had been whether cancer of the tongue was infectious and they should buy a new set of forks and spoons for their office dining-room to avoid the ones he had used. I was interviewed by his partner, now sole head of the firm, Arthur Stockley. He at once laid down the law, in the firmest, even harshest, manner. He clearly disliked and disapproved of my father's mistress,

had no intention of letting her into any spoils, or of sub-
mitting to the sentimental blackmail, as he regarded it,
of my father's blithe and unbusinesslike assumptions. He
was perfectly clear as to what Elders and Fyffes were prepared to do to help my mother—and what they were not
prepared to do. They would provide her with a pension,
perhaps £500 a year, subject to revision at the end of ten
years, but only on condition that my father's wishes with
regard to his mistress were entirely ignored. If I handed over
to her the insurance policy of £2000, my mother, so far as
they were concerned, would get nothing.

Even now I don't see what else I could have done in the
face of this ultimatum but acquiesce. I had only just joined
the BBC, on a salary, so far as I remember, of £350 and could
hardly help my mother much on that; my sister and her
infant child were now on our backs (she had been with us
for a year or more, declining to rejoin her husband in
Panama because of my father's health, until the husband,
losing patience with her prolonged absence, instituted
proceedings for divorce and the long legal struggle for
alimony, which it fell upon me to conduct, was soon to
begin); my mother, who was sixty-five, was used to a
standard of living in which worry about money played no
part; even on what she now stood to get she would have to
be cautioned to be careful, and a new bogey would be
added to her considerable collection of bogeys, as indeed
it was ('I'm not overdrawn, am I? I do try so hard to be
careful and keep within my means'); my duty, I had no
doubt of it, was to her; I regretfully dishonoured my
father's posthumous wishes. This dilemma in which I had
been put I communicated to my father's mistress in her

Castelnau house; of that interview I now recall nothing whatever, but my notebook tells me that I undertook to pay her youngest daughter's school bill.

She had been shrewd in her prognosis in my father's death-chamber: I never saw her again and had no further part in the life of her family, my three half-sisters, until many years had passed. Indeed it would be true to say that I gave them all scarcely another thought. Reasons, good or bad, can easily be marshalled: excepting for the youngest girl, whom I had met only once and quite recently, they were strangers to me; they were a secret, my father's secret, kept from me for over twenty years, and a secret which I had already decided to hide from my mother; they did not yet know of my relationship with them; I felt no interest or curiosity about them; I was leading a homosexual life, totally indifferent to girls, my own sister was worry enough with her disastrous affairs and her frequent jealous warfare with my mother, I had certainly no welcome in my heart for any more sisters; they were of an age to fend for themselves, as I would now have to fend for myself and my family; the house in Castelnau belonged to them, a considerable asset, while our own house in Richmond was rented.

During these transactions with Stockley he said to me, 'By the way, your father's desk is now your property. If you take my advice, you will let me have it burnt with all its contents.' I said, 'All right.' This was a decision I was to regret in later life more than anything else, more, perhaps, than my failure to keep in touch with my half-sisters, with whom I had in the end a close and happy relationship; indeed I regard it now with such astonishment and horror that I can scarcely believe I ever agreed to such an act.

Why did I agree? My then state of mind is so hard to recall that I can only suppose that no problem was in fact posed. I can't even remember what I thought Stockley to mean. He must have meant either that the desk might be contaminated with my father's diseases, or that it contained private papers and letters unfit for filial eyes to see. If the latter, my high-minded state of desiring to honour his posthumous wishes may have included a sense of scruple in invading further the secrets of a life he had not thought fit to share with me. But perhaps the most likely formula for my feelings would be: I was then quite incurious about my father's history; I didn't want his gigantic roll-top desk, what on earth could I do with it?; I was grateful to Stockley for propping my mother up—and I was frightened of him. I have said elsewhere that I was subservient to personalities stronger than my own, and of all my father's 'men pals' Arthur Stockley alarmed me most. A cold, ruthless, self-righteous figure, his unsmiling critical gaze seemed always trying to solve me as though I were a riddle, an unpleasant riddle, for I never felt he liked me. He was, to me, an unnerving man, and if he had said to me instead, 'The desk is yours, take it away', I would have taken it away. The mind which he managed always to enfeeble would have agreed with whatever he said. What the desk contained I have no idea; my father kept no papers at home; if he kept any at all they must have been in it, and it might well have yielded that information about his past life which this memoir so sadly lacks.

Fifteen

To how many other people besides his office cronies was this double life of my father's known? I believe that Dr Wadd was in the secret, and if the discreet Mr Morland, the chauffeur, who waited so often with his car outside the house in Castelnau had not been actually taken into my father's confidence, he had put two and two together from his observations. Only we, his family, remained in the dark, and my mother died seventeen years later, in 1946, in ignorance of his deception. It was therefore, as I said at the beginning of this memoir, one of life's little ironies that her sister, my Aunt Bunny, who lived with and on her after the 'Doc' had followed my father to the grave, and sometimes tried to gain prestige and credit for her diplomatic success in 1919 which rang my mother's marriage bells, was morally precluded from using the sensational and clinching proof of her case which had come to her knowledge ten years later. For prior to 1919, of course, my father was simply a bachelor keeping two mistresses, my mother and Muriel, each with a family of three; had he continued thus and died intestate a complex situation would have arisen.

This second family of my father's, about whose lives I learnt long after his death when I met them, was laid down with twin girls in 1910 when I was a preparatory schoolboy of fourteen. A stillborn boy was said to have preceded them. The third girl was born two years later, round about the time when my father delivered his man-to-man homily to my brother and me in the billiard-room of Grafton House. They were accidents like ourselves. The birth of the twins was registered by him under an assumed name, he borrowed the name of his mistress; the youngest girl was never registered at all. They were all stowed away in a house near Barnes Common in care of the Miss Coutts he mentioned in one of his posthumous letters to me, a doctor's sister and an old confidante of his. Through dietary ignorance or a desire to save his pocket, she fed them so frugally and injudiciously that they all developed rickets. They had no parental care, no family life, no friends. Their mother, whom they did not love or even like, for she had less feeling for them than for her career and reputation, seldom appeared; the youngest girl does not remember to have seen her at all until she was some ten years old. This period contained the war years and the aftermath of war, when the mother was engaged in her active service ambulance work and was therefore much abroad. But three or four times a year a relative of theirs, whom they knew as Uncle Bodger and who jokingly called himself William Whiteley, the Universal Provider, would arrive laden with presents. This gentleman, almost their only visitor, they adored. He would come in a taxi with his load of gifts (sometimes with a dog named Ginger, who had perhaps provided him with a pretext for the visit: 'I'm taking the dog for a walk', and who, since he was *our* dog, was also therefore another conspirator in my father's affairs, had he but known it), and this was the most exciting event in the lonely and unhappy monotony of these young lives. Before he left they would decorate his grey felt hat with wild flowers, sticking them all round its black band, then see him off into his train or bus, from which, as it departed for Richmond, he would wave them goodbye with his garlanded hat. What did he do with the flowers then, I wonder? He could not return to my mother in this festive state. Did he pull them out and throw them away, or make a little posy of them for his dressing table? Visited rather more by their mother and Uncle Bodger in the 'twenties, the girls remained in this house, getting their schooling in Putney and Wimbledon, until my father set them all up in the Castelnau house. Here he was able to see them frequently, for the house lay on the main route between Richmond and his Bow Street office and, travelling now always by Mr Morland's car, he could drop in on them daily during the last two years of his life. They lived therefore, this secret family of his, for nineteen years within easy walking distance of ourselves in Richmond. How often he manged to meet their mother, or where, during this long period I don't know; she may have been at the end of some of those business trips to the Midlands before and after the war; perhaps she was in Paris when I sat with him in the Bois de Boulogne; she certainly went with him on his annual cures to Bad Gastein, which accounts for his startled and cool reception of my compassionate offer to accompany him on the last of these 'lonely' holidays. The prolonged concealment of his paternity of the children seems to have been insisted on by him rather than by her; a time came when they began to get curious and she wanted them told, but he would not allow it, even when he was cracking up. Indeed as they grew into adolescence the anomaly of their situation, their strange, lonely upbringing

[162]

in care of their old woman guardian, the occasional *prima-donna* visits of their unloving and unlovable mother, their lack of a father and their true relationship with the charming and mysterious Uncle Bodger, became a matter, between the twins at least, for discussion, speculation and suspicion. One of them finally, in an emotional state and determined upon the truth, paid him a surprise visit at his office and said to him earnestly, 'Please tell me, are you our father?' His reply, since it was not a denial, seems almost an admission: 'I can't answer such questions. You must ask your mother.' A sad response to a daughter's heartfelt appeal. They were told the truth only after his death.

The discovery of my father's duplicity gave me, I suppose, something of a jolt, not severe to a mind as self-centred as mine, but a jolt which gradually intrigued and then engaged my thought more and more as the years passed. It was the kind of shock that people must receive when some old friend, who has just spent with them an apparently normal evening, goes home and puts his head in the gas-oven. The shock, after the shock of death, is the shock to complacency, to self-confidence: the old friend was a stranger after all, and where lay the fault in communication? My relationship with my father was in ruins; I had known nothing about him at all. The 'grown man with every sign of a great intelligence' who, in his posthumous letter, had stood before him on the morning of October 21, 1920, the year after his belated secret marriage to my mother, had had, it seemed, insufficient intelligence, then and thereafter, to take him in, to make him out, and to the 'kindly nature towards human frailties' that he had believed me to possess, his own frailties were not entrusted.

All his 'men pals', who deserted him at the end like the proverbial rats on the sinking ship, had been let into his 'secret orchard'. I was to join this group 'only in case of my death'.

Why? The question vaguely teased and discomfited my thought, whenever it turned to him, as time went on, and became at last the *raison d'être* of this examining and self-examining book; not the only *raison d'être*, it must be admitted, for, being a writer, I perceived that I had a good story to tell, a story which, as it ramified, grew better and better. If it is true, as I think Arthur Stockley told me, that my father originally met his second mistress at the Tavistock Hotel, the pub in Covent Garden to which they all used to repair in the early decades of the business, and where she worked, I believe he said, behind the bar, his 'men pals' may have got into his 'secret orchard' only because they could not be kept out of it. After all, he had managed to exclude them for many years from that first secret orchard, in Cheshire, in which my mother and ourselves dwelt, until it was accidentally discovered. Nevertheless, since so many trespassers had already got into his second orchard, why was I kept out? Why did he, a businessman, with cherished monetary dispositions on his mind, prefer to leave them to the uncertainty of posthumous letters instead of enlisting my co-operation face to face? It may of course be that, having got so far undetected by us, he hoped to scrape through. As I have already said, I don't know how aware he was of the gravity of his condition; with tickets for Bad Gastein in his pocket he clearly did not expect to die so soon, and his mistress, who did not know the nature of his complaint, certainly hoped that if she

could only get him to his spa she might recover him. Some
such optimism may have buoyed them up and, after all,
more perhaps by good luck than good management,
they had almost brought the thing off, the 'secret orchard'
had preserved its secret from us for nearly twenty years,
my sister was well married and off his hands (or so he
thought; her divorce proceedings were instituted after his
death), I had my job in the BBC, his three other girls had
practically reached marriageable or working age, success
was almost within his grasp; given a little more luck, a
little more life, he may have thought, and he would be
rid of the expense of five children, all launched upon the
world, and be able to destroy his letters to me, leaving his
secret forever undisclosed. Yet of course this only begs the
question of why he preferred to exclude me from his
confidence—and why, for that matter, he preferred to
exclude his three daughters also. Did he enjoy secretiveness
for its own sake? His history abounds in instances of it.
Or was he ashamed? Could he have conceived that, so
far as I was concerned and in spite of my 'kindly nature
towards human frailties', I would have been morally
shocked, embarrassed, even censorious? Did he think I
would reproach him? Indeed I *would* have reproached him
—for failing, in the chance he had, to provide me with
some more brothers instead of all those extra sisters.
What a thrilling present that would have seemed to me
then, some brand-new, teen-age brothers! They might
even have yielded the Ideal Friend! How *could* he have
viewed me, this ex-guardsman with his 'secret orchards'
and way of life as shady as my own? My half-sisters believed that he and their mother, who also met my sailor in

Southsea, realised that I was 'queer', but they could not have known that I was a practising homosexual, and I wonder whether, with my 'highbrow' intellectuality, my lack of interest in girls, my obvious preference for the company of working-class 'lads', I could so have fogged him, so have presented myself to him, that he supposed me to be a sort of social worker, an idealist, a selfless, high-minded fellow remote from and superior to himself. I have reason to believe that I often wear a frown. Our public faces can be known to us only by hearsay and I have been given several clues to my own. A preoccupied anxious look seems to be my most settled guise, tinged by sadness. A charming smile: 'sunshine through tears', someone once described it to me. My fine blue eyes can emit a piercing stare, I am told, though what on earth they pierce I have no notion, they certainly did not manage to pierce my father. And, as I say, a frown may darken my face. My mother would sometimes make it worse by trying to smooth it away with her fingers. 'It will spoil your beautiful brows,' she said. I was told later, to my sorrow, that love me though she did she was rather scared of me ('Do you lov your little mother?' she would say, as though the full word were too much to ask for), and I expect I gave her cause; with her ceaseless chatter she invited defence, the raised barricading newspaper, the yawn, the frown, the off-hand manner, the bored, inattentive face. A friend once remarked to me, 'It's wonderful how rude one can be to your mother without her even noticing it.' It may be, therefore, that if I contrived to scare her off with my frowning, preoccupied look, I scared my father too. Perhaps he found my 'piercing' eyes

as disconcerting as I found his squinty ones. I set it down for
what it may be worth.

Mention of my mother brings me to another question:
did my father fear that if I were allowed into his 'secret
orchard', she, by way of indiscretion, might get a look-in
too? This could be, though it does not explain that other
secrecy he maintained towards his daughters. Yet I have a
deep conviction that had my brother been alive he would,
sooner or later, have been included among the 'men pals'.
I don't see my father as a cunning, or even a clever, man
(the muddlement in Southsea was pure French farce),
and the surprising thing is that considering how much he
must surely have fibbed to my mother at the beginning
of his affair and over all those Richmond years when we
were at school and she and my grandmother (who continued to live with us until her death in 1917 and whom he
loved and respected) had him under observation, and considering how well instructed they both already were in his
ways and the ways of the world, and considering how many
other people with whom my mother was also acquainted
were 'in the know'— the surprising thing is that she never
suspected or got wind of anything. I say 'suspected' without knowledge; how much uneasiness (apart from her lack
of marital status), if any, he caused her during my schooldays when he was busy laying down his second family,
I am unable to tell; I can only say that, excepting for two
strange episodes, my parents seemed, to my boy mind,
during my holidays, to be leading happy and harmonious
lives. To one of these episodes I shall come shortly; the
other was a shocking struggle over *Webster's Dictionary*. I
can assign no date to this, but my recollection is that some

word, its spelling or meaning, was in hot dispute between my parents and both determined to look it up and say, 'I told you so'. My father commanded my mother to fetch the dictionary, which was in the library; when she was slow in returning with it he guessed she was consulting it herself. Rushing out after her he wrenched the heavy volume from her hands in a violent struggle that left her weeping on the floor. I remember no more about it, and it is the only instance of their quarrelling that I recall. But I don't recall either how much of my father, in that pre-war Richmond decade, *c.* 1904–1914, we all saw or expected to see. Living with us though he then was, I believe that business excuses of various sorts, received by my gullible mother as an accepted though disappointing matter of course, took him often from our midst; he seldom, if ever, for instance, accompanied us on our summer holidays to the seaside; it was only in the post-war decade 1919–1929 that I picture him as the constant paterfamilias, the regular commuter. In the pre-war period of his liaison I expect he must have felt himself to be in something of a mess, but as the years of deception rolled successfully by, and especially after he married my mother in 1919, I wonder to what extent he continued to worry about secrecy—and to what extent she would have minded had she found him out.

I have used the word 'jealousy' in connection with her in this memoir. My Aunt Bunny used to say that she was very jealous in her youth, and my sister accused her of jealousy throughout their tormented lives together. My mother, as *I* recall her, was not a jealous woman, her mind was too capricious, her disposition too generous and un-demanding, to harbour the emotion. Some small degree of

jealousy she may have had; she was incapable of sulking
or of nursing resentments. Had she learnt of my father's
duplicity when we learnt of it, she would have been as
astounded as we were, it was on so grand a scale, indeed
it took one's breath away, and if you take people's breath
away much else goes with it. Retrospective memory is
flummoxed, tears become absurd, recrimination knows not
where to begin; what *was* there to say? and I believe that
my mother, when her rambling, preoccupied mind had
managed to take the staggering *fait accompli* in, would have
got used to living with it as with a new parlour-maid or a
new hat. I think she would have been curious to see his
three daughters, and charming to them of course as she
was charming to everyone. In fact I have sometimes regretted that I kept her in the dark, as I have regretted losing
touch for so long with the other family; had I acted otherwise and brought us all together at once, the last seventeen
years of my mother's life might have been less dull and
lonely. And, after all, was anyone ever so affectionately
deceived? Whatever my father's mistress received from
him in the way of love, thought and attention, *she*, at any
rate in the 'twenties, the decade in which I visualise them
best, could have had no sense of neglect. He had for her the
sweetest, tenderest feelings. Indeed the thing that might
have puzzled her most, a thing hardly to be credited, was
that someone who had belonged to her so fully could
possibly have found time to belong to anyone else. Fully?
Here again I can only conjecture, but if my conjecture is
right I think she must have taken that too into consideration
in any view of his behaviour; I conjecture that in the matter
of sex my father let her off it, at her request, quite early in

their married life—and had to look for it elsewhere. She was the most nervous of women and never ceased to complain of her three confinements, of the pains and hardships she had endured, the subsequent illnesses, puerperal fevers, prostrations. Child-bearing had been for her unqualified misery and suffering, and my guess is that soon after my sister's birth she began to excuse herself from the marriage bed. As I have said, she became at last what we called 'a chemist's delight'.

The other disharmonious event I have mentioned as belonging to my schooldays, a curious, tragical episode in her story, may help to illumine her character and her relations with my father. At about the same time that he was embarking upon his liaison with his mistress, she made a gentleman friend. Harold Armstrong had been a rubber planter in Sumatra. A smallish, paunchy, balding middle-aged man, with a blunt tip to his long nose and rather splay feet, we met him during a seaside holiday in Lowestoft or Margate. I was a preparatory schoolboy and recall that I never felt quite at ease with him, sensing that he did not like me much, or as much as my brother, to whom he wrote far longer letters in his sloping hand. This man fell in love with my mother, he would have married her if he could. She used to say that they were 'soul mates', and I believe they were, more than she and my father had ever been or ever could be. *His* love for her was of a compassionate, tender, sheltering kind, the sort of love we feel for a small, nervous animal: indeed he called her 'the Rat' and had the line-image of a rat, as drawn by herself, engraved upon the silver backs of her hair-brushes and other toilet utensils, because she hoarded things up; if anything in the house was missing it was sure to be found in her room. But Harold Armstrong was her *alter ego*, he appealed to something fundamental in her, her reality, the little girl in her nature, she could be herself with him. The world they inhabited together was a fairy-tale world of pure romance and eternal youth; all her jokes and foibles, which often seemed to us so silly, had for him the utmost charm, he laughed with her, not at her as we did; they invented a private childish language between themselves (her boudoir in Grafton House, for instance, was known to them as 'the P. J. room'—which stood for 'the Private Jaw room'); he called her 'Little Lady' and always kissed her hand.

He became a frequent visitor to the house and, outwardly at least, got along amicably with my father, but I fancy that the latter was disturbed by this friendship. I was too young to understand the rest of this matter, but I believe that Armstrong was in some financial strait and asked my father for employment in Elders and Fyffes. His request was refused, and perhaps because he was generally lonely and frustrated and saw no endurable future, he committed suicide in a Reading hotel. Standing before the mirror in his bedroom he watched himself put the muzzle of the revolver into his mouth: this much was reconstructed by the police from the position in which he was found, fallen forward over the dressing table. My father, I remember, called us children together and said to us gravely, 'Be particularly kind to your little mother.' In later years we were not kind; when she spoke of Armstrong, as she sometimes did, we would pretend to believe in our teasing way that there had been more to this friendship than the 'purely platonic romance' she always vehemently asserted and which I have no doubt was the truth. One evening she burst into tears at our beastliness and fled from the room. How deeply she cared for this man I do not know, or how deeply she was capable of caring for anyone: it is a question that applies as unanswerably to myself.

She did not appear to miss my father when he died, I don't recall her grieving for him; she seldom spoke of him and no photographs of him, as I remember, stood about Blenheim House or the smaller house, in Sheen Road, to which I afterwards moved her. In this respect she differed from Aunt Bunny who, up to the day of her death at the age of ninety-three, kept always on her bedside table a photo of the detestable 'Doc' and hoped she would be so blessed as to be able to warm his carpet slippers for him in Heaven too. *She*, I am sure, would have been profoundly upset if, after his death, there had been revelations of his infidelity to her, indeed she would have refused them credence, however damning the evidence, her loyalty to her unworthy old friends and her need for devotion being so great. But my mother had no conception of religion and gave no thought to an after-life. To consider the life after death naturally involves envisaging death, a perfectly horrid subject, and she regarded such heavenly hopes as her sister entertained as extremely unhealthy and what she called 'morbid'. To stay alive and well was problem enough for her, and the recipe for that was to keep the bowels open, to try to be cheerful and light-hearted, to take plenty of exercise (inside the house was safer than outside), not to lean out of railway-carriage windows, or spill the salt, or walk under ladders, to hide the knives and drape the mirrors at the approach of thunderstorms, and always to

spit if there was a bad smell. One of my few early recollections of her is raising her veil to spit vigorously in the
street, exhorting us to do likewise. I remember too a time
when, before going to sleep, she would place her loose cash
and rings on a chair outside her bedroom door, together
with a note to burglars generally, which read: 'Take my
money but spare our lives.' She wrote always with a quill,
a large dashing hand, full of exclamation marks and under-
linings.

I believe, therefore, that long ago, at the beginning of the
century, she had managed to disengage herself from the
sexual embraces of my father, that large heavy man whose
weight upon her small nervous organism must have been
crushing, and that she would have adjusted her mind, such
as it was, to the knowledge that some other woman had
been bearing the burden she had renounced, even though
the 'peccadillo'—a word she used—had resulted in three
more children. What concerned her, and continued to
concern her without cause, was not the disappearance of
her 'dear old Punch' from her scene, but her financial
situation as his widow. She was a woman entirely without
skills or the common leisure occupations of her generation;
although she had devised our menus throughout our lives,
her housekeeping was always conducted through a staff
of servants; she could not knit or sew (Aunt Bunny and
their mother were fine needlewomen); her piano, to which
she had once turned for amusement, was gradually given
up; avoiding the horrors if possible, she read nothing but
the newspapers, chiefly for the racing news (she put small
bets on horses, selecting them for the personal appeal of
their names), prize competitions and crossword puzzles,

at which Aunt Bunny was far cleverer than she; she played
patience, chattered exhaustingly on the telephone or to her
female helps or visitors, seldom left her small house except
for little toddles round the corner with her current Sealyham and, in the late 'thirties, took secretly to the bottle.
Ending up as I am with animals and alcohol, one of her
last friends, when she was losing her faculties, was a fly,
which I never saw but which she talked about a good deal
and also talked to. With large melancholy yellow eyes and
long lashes it inhabited the bathroom; she made a little
joke of it but was serious enough to take in crumbs of bread
every morning to feed it, scattering them along the wooden
rim of the bath as she lay in it, much to the annoyance of
Aunt Bunny who had to clear up after her. Apart from my
continual intervention in the wretched warfare that was
waged between her and my sister, of which I had to bear
the tell-tale brunt from both sides, I don't remember ever
having had a serious, intimate conversation with my
mother in my life; yet when I think of her, as I sometimes
do, or look at her photos with that sad face she always
put on for photographers, I take much of her psychology to
myself.

I have now put down a number of possible reasons to
account for my father's decision to exclude me from his
confidence. The word 'decision' may be queried as too
definite; it is very probable that, after a time, as in his long
irregular life with my mother, he ceased to bother himself.
Had he wished to consult me in his affairs, he could not
have done so until 1919, the year when I was back from the
war and had come of age, and although this was also the
year of his marriage to my mother, so that some tidying

up got done, I daresay that by then a good deal of *laissez-faire* and laziness had set in. Things with him had always slid, he let them slide—they seemed usually to slide the way he wanted—not exerting himself, muddling along, hoping for the best. Good-humoured, easy-going, tolerant, his motto, I imagine, was 'Live and let live' in this 'wonderful old world'. Yet when he took up his pen to write to me in 1920, again in 1927, he made decisions; he decided, for some reason, that in this posthumous way, and not by personal interview, I was to be informed and instructed.

When I started this memoir, in the 'thirties, my inclination was to blame myself for this failure in communication, indeed I still do not let myself off; inattentive always, I simply did not attend to him, he was my good old father who kept me comfortably and independently on my feet and sent down cases of champagne every year for my boatrace parties in Hammersmith, to which he himself, though invited, never came; beyond that, except in the matter of health, I never gave him a thought. How should one expect confidence from a person whom one regards more as a useful piece of furniture than as a human being? Yet that is all very well. If I took no interest in him, he did not make himself of much interest to me. He was, after all, my senior and a man of the world, incidentally my father; whatever the obstacles, any move towards a closer relationship should have come from his responsible and more experienced side, and he could easily have captured me had he wished; he had only to ask me to lunch or dine with him alone at Romano's and say, 'Look here, Joe, you're a selfish fellow, wrapped up in your own affairs, but I have something important to tell you and would like your attention for a change.' To such an approach I, the natural subordinate, would have been readily, agreeably open: either he did not realise this, or could not make it, or did not want it. This brings me to my last account with him.

Sixteen

In 1925 I took a flat in Hammersmith. The river front, seen from the bridge as I drove between Richmond and London in my car, had caught my fancy and determined me to live there; I often explored it but found nothing to let. Then one day a small shopkeeper near Hammersmith Terrace, a charming row of eighteenth-century houses, said that he believed that the owners of No. 6 had some unused rooms and were thinking of taking a lodger. The name was Needham. I at once called at No. 6. A tall, heavy, untidy man of about sixty, clad in a dressing-gown over shirt and trousers, opened the door to me. He seemed taken aback and flustered by my enquiry. It was true there was an unused floor in the house, true he had been thinking of letting it, but he had not made up his mind, the place was not ready, he had never had a lodger before, he was not perfectly sure that he wanted one, he could not understand how the matter had 'got about'. Nevertheless he was friendly and kept saying 'Good gracious me!' with a titter, shielding his mouth with his hand as he spoke. I asked to see the rooms and he consented. They were empty, grubby, but charming, a self-contained flat on the first floor overlooking the river which flowed at the bottom of the small garden, the very thing I wanted. I persuaded him to rent them to me and in due course moved in.

I was a serious, rather severe, young man, making no progress with my writing and hampered by a lack of confidence in myself, some inkling perhaps of incapacity. My poetic drama about Galeazzo Maria Sforza, of which there was practically nothing to show but some mawkish speeches between the two young conspirators on the eve of the assassination, had been irritably abandoned, and I was toying with a new play, *Judcote* (the name of the house of a family called Jude), which required no research, being based upon the exasperatingly stupid and monotonous home life in Richmond from which I had again escaped. Little did I then know that beneath the surface of that dull domestic scene lay concealed a plot every whit as sensational and dramatic as anything I could devise. The plot of *Judcote* (never finished) scarcely needs description, it can be guessed: a young, upper-middle-class, intellectual homosexual (myself of course), lonely, frustrated, and sick of his family, especially the women, his feckless chatterbox of a mother, his vain, quarrelsome and extravagant sister, and the general emptiness and futility of their richly upholstered life, becomes emotionally involved with a handsome young workman. This workman and his mate come to repair the french windows of the Judes' sitting-room, the catch of which has broken, so that they are always drifting open, being irritably closed, drifting open again (symbolism, you see, the invitation to escape), and the young Jude catches envious sight of the two young men affectionately larking at their work. The larking ends in a small disaster, for the handsome boy's chisel accidentally wounds the hand of his mate. But Jude has had a vision of the happy companionship he lacks. Months later the windows start drifting open again, manual labour is once more summoned, only the handsome boy turns up.

Where is his mate? asks Jude. Dead of course, the cut in his hand turned septic and he died of septicaemia. Jude bursts into tears. The boy puts his arm round him and comforts him. Jude falls in love with him and, after various other happenings which I never got right, runs away with him into a working-class life and they live happily together as mates ever after. When this romantic play declined to budge, as it constantly did, I had my Indian notebooks to fall back on.

My main neurosis at this time was noise. The need for undisturbed quietness throughout the working day had become an obsession with me, upon the lack of it I blamed my failure as a writer, and in my preliminary negotiations with Mr Arthur Needham I particularly stressed this point: was his house quiet? should I be plagued with noises—pianos, radios, gramophones, voices—from within or through the walls from the neighbours on either side? Nervously he reassured me, the house was as quiet as the grave; he could hardly have foreseen the cause of my eventual exasperation. In retrospect it amuses me to think that a noise which now seems to me so jolly and sympathetic, then enraged me: the barking of dogs. During my six or seven years in this flat I became a querulous dog-denouncer. Whenever the tide was low, local residents would take their dogs on to the foreshore of the river and excite them to a constant yapping by throwing sticks into the water for them to retrieve. This got on my nerves to such an extent that as soon as yapping started, even if it were so far off as to be only faintly heard, I would utter a groan or curse, push aside my play and wearily bring out my Indian journal instead, a task which I regarded as akin to idleness, an admission of failure, since my extensive notebooks already supplied its rough material and to present it required no great concentration or inspiration. *Hindoo Holiday*, therefore, which has sometimes been dubbed a classic, was largely written in a spirit of vexation. I now know that had the house been indeed as quiet as the grave I should never have completed my play, or any other play; my inventive ability and (more important) my power of application were too slight.

Another allied foible was the conviction that one should discourage familiarity with anyone whose proximity—landlord, neighbour, other lodger—lent him a possible nuisance value. In one of my previous flats, of which my tenancies had been transient, my landlady, a 'plump little partridge' if ever there was one, had at last managed through her tireless concern for my comfort, her constant knocking on my door to ask if I had everything I wanted, to dislodge me, and I was therefore determined to keep the Needhams at bay. There were three of them, Mr Arthur, his brother Cecil, and their sister Louie: they must have thought me an extremely brusque and unsociable fellow. Having already unnerved poor Arthur with my strictures over noise, so that he crept about his own house like a mouse, I then managed, for some eighteen months or two years, to give an impression of such urgent busyness as, with precipitate haste and the most perfunctory of salutations, I flew past the Needhams in the hallway, on the stairs, that soon they slid nervously out of the way whenever I was heard approaching; there would be a sound of scurry, a sense of rapidly disappearing figures and quietly closing doors. As with the hidden plot in my Richmond home, little did I know what I was missing here too. But as time passed and I perceived that my privacy had nothing to fear from these old people, moreover that I should never make of that privacy any literary use, my defences were gradually relaxed and I began to take an interest in this strange, eccentric, Dickensian trio.

They were all bachelors, the offspring of that J. Needham who has a notable place in the *Encyclopaedia Britannica* (Eleventh Edition) under the subject 'GUN'. In 1874 he had invented 'the ejector mechanism by which each empty cartridge case is separately and automatically thrown out of the gun when the breach is opened'. Mr Arthur and Mr Cecil (known as 'Cis') had followed in his footsteps, Arthur as inventor, Cis as executor; but cigarettes and water instead of cartridges were the objects now ejected from their contrivances. They had made and patented a round metal cigarette-box and a cigarette-case, called respectively the 'Pick-me-up Container' and the 'Take-one Case', which, either by being lifted, or pressed or slid in some part of their anatomy, automatically poked up a cigarette into your hand to save you the fatigue of selecting one for yourself. Their other invention was a Perpetual Fountain, designed to stand amid ferns on the dining table, or to hang as a lamp from the ceiling, which forever sprayed up and retrieved its own small internal puddle of water and was said to be in some demand among Eastern potentates and fishmongers.

These articles were made by Cis, with the assistance of a spotty little boy, actually on the premises, or, rather, under them, in a workshop beneath the garden. There, in this subterranean chamber, among packing cases, tools, lathes, and antediluvian machinery, he spent practically the whole of his conscious life, bent over his benches, his steel spectacles tied at the back of his head with a piece of string to prevent them falling off into the baths of acid and solder. A *farouche*, unshaven, grimy, wiry little terrier of a man, whose unkempt hair sprouted as profusely from his brows and ears as from his head, he seldom rose to the surface, except to rush stealthily from time to time down the garden (as I observed from my window) to take by surprise, if he could, the mischievous little ragamuffins who prowled the foreshore when the tide was out and enjoyed to clamber upon and rock his grounded sailing boat which was tethered to the garden wall. This boat, his cigarette-cases and perpetual fountains were the loves of his life (he had had no sexual experience of any kind, Mr Arthur, who had lived with him always, informed me later), and when I got to know him better he took me for a sail or two.

Miss Louie too was seldom seen. A tall old woman of nearly seventy she looked after her brothers to whom she was devoted, as they to her, and had become almost a part of the dust and dinge of the cluttered house against which she was no longer able to prevail. Beneath the thin white hair her scalp was visibly grey with dirt, as also were her feeble fluttering hands. Yet once upon a time, one saw, she must have been pretty, this emaciated, nervous, faded old woman, whose dentures clicked and trembled as she spoke; a spectral beauty remained. She too from my window I sometimes saw in the garden, ineffectually poking and striking with a walking-stick at the stray cats who came in from neighbouring gardens to crouch on the walls or the trellised arch that carried her rambler roses in wait for the birds towards whom her sympathies lay. 'Go away, cruel, cruel creatures!' she would cry in a quavering voice, striking, thwack, thwack at the astonished pussy-cats, 'Go away, you horrid cruel things!'

The only other occupant of the house was a large brown dog named Prince, so old that *rigor mortis* seemed already to be setting in. If he managed to totter stiffly out to the nearest tree in the garden, he seldom accomplished his purpose of lifting his leg against it. Peering frowningly down at him from my window, in these dog-denouncing days, I would observe him with horror straining with feeble persistence to hoist his leg without over-balancing. How kind I would be to him now! I would lift his old leg for him. He smelt from afar of his own approaching death; the lower part of the house was always rank with this odour of decay, mingled with the peculiar smells that arose from Cis's workshop beneath the garden.

The use of this garden was available to me also, though I did not enter it much, at any rate during the time when I was avoiding the Needhams. To reach it one had to pass through their drawing-room, as I suppose it might be called, a large ground-floor room they never used themselves, preferring a small parlour that opened off it. This large room, into which I sometimes peeped when the coast seemed clear, was like a junk shop, crammed with dusty furniture, occasional tables, screens and relics of the Needhams' past. Its walls were plastered with pictures, portraits, photographs and framed diplomas, foxed and faded like their owners. The walls of the staircase too, up and down which I dashed in my evasive days, were thickly hung with the overflow of these pictures and testimonials; among them, I sometimes noticed as I hastened by, was a particularly large amateurish oil-painting of a pompous old gentleman dressed in ceremonial attire and seated on a kind of throne. He had bulging blue eyes and a large moustache that extended beyond the sides of his face and, waxed at the points, turned upwards like the Kaiser's. A pale aristocratic hand, issuing from the folds of his vice-regal robes, rested on the arm of his throne. How was I to know that this old gentleman was the Count James Francis de Gallatin, my father's boyhood friend?

'I thought you was never going to speak to me,' said old Arthur Needham reproachfully one day when we were becoming pally and confidential. Of the trio he was the one most frequently met with. His inventive fancies having long since exhausted themselves over the creation of the Pick-me-up Container, the Take-one Case, and the Perpetual Fountain, his life's work was done; short of occupation and breath he was often to be found wheezing bronchially about the passages, unshaven, clad in his habitual dressing-gown, his collarless shirt fastened at the throat with a brass stud. His scanty grey hair had been doctored, obviously by himself, no barber could have made such a mess of it; aspiring to be blond, it was almost orange at the sides. Met in this négligé, when the thaw between us was setting in, he was always overcome by a genteel, simpering embarrassment: 'Fancy you catching me like this!' His fluster was greater if, as often happened, he was not wearing his dentures—'me ornaments' he called them—and he would shield his mouth with his hand, apologising from behind it with few aitches and much old-maidish giggling. How easy it is to make fun of old people and old animals! Forty years later I myself, with one tooth only in my upper jaw, do much the same as old Arthur did: my denture bothers me, I carry it in my pocket when I am not eating and try to restore it unobserved to my mouth if I meet some friend unexpectedly in the street.

Probably from the very beginning, when I first pressed the bell of No. 6 Hammersmith Terrace and Arthur Needham opened the door, I divined that he was homosexual, or as we put it, 'one of us', 'that way', 'so', or 'queer'. One soon got a sense for such recognitions. But with my fear of interruptions and distractions I did not wish to know more, certainly not to claim kinship with him. The intellectual policeman I have already mentioned helped to bring about the happy result of the closer relationship I had hitherto stifled. Recognising me one evening when he was on duty in King Street as the author of *The Prisoners of War*, which had lately been produced and he had seen, he became a friend of mine and got me going socially in Hammersmith much faster than I could ever have got on by myself. Soon No. 6 was being visited by him and other policemen, his selected friends, as well as by sundry pet tradesboys and costermongers whom he had discovered in the course of his day or night duties. Old Arthur, whose lair was on the ground floor, would often answer the bell (I had no bell of my own) and, after the first shock of finding uniformed policemen on his doorstep, much enjoyed the excitement and vicarious pleasure of admitting these youthful, friendly callers. He himself, I think, had pretty well abdicated whatever active sexual life he had enjoyed; but sometimes he would smarten himself up, put on collar and tie and a complete suit, pop in his 'ornaments' and, assembled in all his parts, issue sedately forth in the evening and proceed, with slow dignified strides of his long thin legs, to his favourite pub in King Street, a tall, erect, distinguished-looking old man, high-shouldered, rather pot-bellied, a walking-stick beneath his arm and, in his jacket pocket, a curious small antique. This, which he gave me before I left, was a silver pin or spike about four inches long, of unknown origin, age, or utility, one end of which was prettily carved in the form of an erect silver penis gripped by a silver hand. The carving, though perfectly realistic, was so delicately done, the composition so neat, that the design was not instantly discernible, a second look, even a third, was needed to recognise it.

With this object, old Arthur said, he had had much fun in his time. Standing beside some 'interesting' young man in a pub and getting into conversation with him about the football or the dogs, he would bring out his pin and ostentatiously excavate with its spiky end the dottle of his pipe, awaiting the query: 'What have you got there?', when he would pass it over for inspection and 'interesting' developments might ensue. It was indeed by means of this trick that he brought my own defences finally down, for I too said, 'What have you got there?' and after that our cards, which the visiting policemen had already started to deal, were all on the table. But by this time, although he still carried his silver pin about for excavating his pipe, Arthur had become a timid and nervous old man, much preoccupied with his health ('Oh dear, isn't it awful to be old?'), and I doubt whether he did much more than stand about in the notorious Hammersmith urinals, of which there were several, hoping for a glimpse of something not made of silver.

That I don't remember when and how the link between my name and the Count de Gallatin's, both uncommon, was first established and my introduction to his portrait performed is not as surprising as it may appear. It certainly occurred before my father's death in 1929, but would not have made upon me any impression stronger than that of an odd coincidence. For it must be clearly understood that, excepting for a few unrelated facts, the story of my father's life as I have set it down here was not then in my head. It was only after his death, and long after his death, that I investigated it, so far as I could, and put it together. I knew he had started as a guardsman; I knew he had had two friends in his youth, and although I might have had to think twice to recall the name of Mr Ashmore, the Count de Gallatin's, perhaps for snob reasons, had stuck in my mind. Vaguely I knew that there had been some unpleasantness between them which had terminated their friendship, though I could not have said what it was, and I was aware of his first marriage to Louise Burckhardt, some of whose ivory toilet things, with 'Louise' engraved upon them, were still used by my mother. That was about the extent of my knowledge. When the ghosts of his past started prowling about me at No. 6 Hammersmith Terrace shortly before he died, I knew little about his life and cared less.

There were two ghosts, one live and one dead. The dead ghost was the Count. So far as I recollect, Arthur asked me, soon after he managed to get at my ear, whether it could have been a relative of mine who, many years ago, had been

a friend of his dear old friend the Count de Gallatin.
Doubtless I said, 'Why, yes, my father. He knew the
Count de Gallatin when he was a young man,' and
thus my formal introduction to the old gentleman of the
portrait was effected. He had lived, it emerged, in a house
just round the corner, No. 3 St. Peter's Square, which
Arthur had found for him and helped him to move into
from Belgravia after Mme de Gallatin's death. There he
was looked after by a man-servant, Tommy, and his
faithful housekeeper, Miss Emily Lenfant, and there
he had died in 1915. He had been for many years a
regular visitor at No. 6, 'Never missed a Sunday,' said
old Arthur.

'Miss Emily', as she was always referred to, was the
living ghost, and I suspect that it was primarily through
her memory rather than Arthur's that the link between the
Count and myself was forged. A Catholic orphan of unknown parentage, she was taken as a child by Mme de
Gallatin from the convent orphanage in which she had been
reared, given the name of Lenfant (*l'Enfant*) and employed
in various capacities, as 'help', lady's maid, and finally
housekeeper. She had known my father at The Hermitage,
Old Windsor, over forty years ago. When Mme de
Gallatin died, she had continued to devote herself to the
Count, until he too died, aged sixty-two, of fatty degenera-
tion of the heart. A woman in the sixties now herself, she
had remained on the friendliest terms with the Needhams,
was a constant visitor to their house, and was to reside in it
and look after the two brothers when Miss Louie died in
1930. It was not until then, the year after my father's
death, that I was introduced to her.

It is probable, therefore, that speculation between Arthur and Miss Emily about a link between the new lodger (myself) and the Count began at No. 6 directly after my arrival. Indeed there may have been no speculation at all; I don't know to what extent Miss Emily was in Mme de Gallatin's and the Count's confidence, but some of the drama had passed before her very eyes, and it seems safe to assume that she would instantly have realised that the young Mr Ackerley who had just rented Arthur's first-floor flat could be none other than the son of that other young Mr Ackerley who broke the Count's heart in 1887 and joined Arthur Stockley (whom also she would have known) in Elders and Fyffes in 1892. In which case, she and old Arthur having easily worked me out, the form of his opening question to me was merely a diffident and tactful way of gaining information he already possessed—and passing it on to me. How galling therefore it must have been for the intrigued and excited old man to have to control his curiosity for so long, owing to my evasive tactics.

The cat out of the bag, his pent-up loquacity was also let loose and I was shown further relics of the Count, gifts and photographs, mostly signed, in which the moustache, though still waxed, did not turn up at the ends but proceeded on to a directer conclusion. I asked if he had ever spoken of my father, and Arthur said yes, once or twice, but 'Oh dear me, you couldn't mention his name! The Count never forgave him for the way he treated him!' Old Arthur, it soon appeared, was a snob, and the words 'the Count' were thereafter frequently on his lips, as also was the name of another noble friend of his, Lord Norton. This old gentleman I was once privileged to meet when I

ran into him and Arthur promenading in the street, a
spruce Nice figure with a silver-headed cane and a flower
in his button-hole.

Later still I was being given to understand, with many a
circumlocution, much tittering, and many fits of coughing,
that of course his friend the Count had also been 'that way',
'Oh my word, very much so'. This could not have surprised me greatly; I had already written off Lord Norton
as another old quean, like Arthur himself, and since we all,
as homosexuals, tended, as with any other persecuted group,
to find our way into the closed and sympathetic society of
our kind, I assumed that Arthur's bosom cronies were
probably as 'queer' as himself. But I was amused and
questioned him: What was the Count like? Oh he was a
charming man with a French accent, but (from my notebooks):

'Good gracious me, he was *awful*! So unscrupulous! I
daren't introduce him to people, heavens no! I introduced a young friend one day and, oh my word! I'd
told the Count that he *wasn't* "that way", but would you
believe it? he asked him round to his house and tried it on
at once! And my young friend said to me afterwards
when I asked him what he thought of the Count, "Well,"
he said, "he seemed a funny sort of chap and I'll tell you
this that if he hadn't been a friend of yours I'd have
punched him on the nose!" Of course I didn't like to say
much to the Count, but I asked him what he'd thought
of my young friend, and he said, "Oh, he seemed quite
nice at first, but then he was *dreadful*!" Goodness me, I
couldn't be seen with him, the way he carried on! There

was another time at the Napoleon! It was *too* much! I didn't know where to look! He simply went straight up to any soldier he fancied!'

I already knew the Napoleon and was to get to know it better and to 'carry on' there myself, though with more circumspection than the Count; it is a pub in Knightbridge, not far from the Horseguards' Barracks, in which my father had once dwelt, a famous resort for picking up cavalrymen. At some point in these confidences I said jokingly to Arthur, 'Do you suppose the Count ever tried anything on with my father?' This put him into such a delicious taking that his bronchials went wrong, and coughing and spluttering, 'Oh my goodness the things you say! Good gracious me, you've quite took me breath away . . .!' he hastened from the room.

Unhappily I made of these conversations with Arthur Needham very few notes. Though amused I was not interested enough and did not foresee how curious I should become later. But I find some other small jottings. He gave me a description of the interior of the Count's St Peter's Square house at which, of course, he was a frequent visitor. The sitting-room, he recalled, contained a full-length portrait of Mme de Gallatin, so painted and placed in an alcove that it gave the illusion that she was approaching through a curtained doorway and about to step down into the room between the ferns that had been carefully arranged to conceal the lower edge of the frame. The Count never kept photos or letters, said Arthur; there were certainly no visible relics of my father, 'Good gracious no'; a snap or two of current soldiers might be found lying about, but the Count always tore them up when the soldiers let him down. 'Dreadfully fat and ugly' in his last years, he was often to be seen in summer time on his verandah in the Square, sitting or parading up and down in a silk dressing-gown, much to the surprise and displeasure of his more conventional neighbours ('Goodness me, the Miss Hughes who lived on the corner, they were *always* complaining, they didn't think it at all *nice*'), who would have been more surprised and displeased had they known what brought him out, which was to examine the tradesboys flying round the Square on their bicycles. When the war broke out, said Arthur, the Count used to take cigarettes to the wounded soldiers in some local hospital ('Oh yes, wherever soldiers were the Count was sure to be'); but his ill luck in friendship, begun by my father, apparently pursued him throughout his life; even Tommy, his ex-guardsman servant, let him down at last. 'A young "so" man', picked up by Arthur in a Hyde Park urinal and subsequently annexed by the Count, he instantly decamped after his master's death and almost before he was cold, with everything portable in the house he could lay hands on and vanished ('Oh, isn't it shocking!'). Having got through three fortunes in his life according to Arthur Stockley, the Count died worth £128. os. 4d., but he had also some property in America, and this and everything else that Tommy did not pinch was inherited by the faithful Miss Emily.

Seventeen

THIS story, dropped into my ears whenever Arthur could gain access to them, took some time to unfold, and so much longer to impress itself that I am vague now about dates and the sequence of events. I reached No. 6, as I have said, in 1925, my father died in the autumn of 1929, it was not until at least half-way through that period that I was introduced to the portrait of the Count de Gallatin. How much of the scandalous information about him I received before my father died I don't recall, nor does it matter; had I had it all, as maybe I did, it would have made no difference to my thought and behaviour. The story was odd, it was amusing, it had, so far as my father was concerned, absolutely no reality. It must be understood that he was at this time the father-figure I have described in my Chapters 8–10. The story of his double life was not yet disclosed, nor the story of his dealings with my mother, which came later; he was simply my old familiar dad, with his large top-heavy figure, his Elder Statesman look, his Edward VII hat, umbrella, and eternal cigar, his paunch, his moustache, his swivel eye, his jumps and his unsteady gait, his dull commuting, respectable life, his important business, his dreary office pals, and their eternal yarning about chaps putting their hands up girls' frocks (never into boys' flies)—it was difficult enough as I have said, to think of him in any amorous situation at all; to imagine him in the arms of another man was not possible. It must be added that, besides my ignorance of his history, I had not yet seen the photos of him as a young man which illustrate this book; they came into my hands years later from Uncle Denton and Stockley; the only early photo of him in the family album that I recollect was the New Brighton group on the lion-skin rug, an innocent looking affair, if only because there was safety in numbers.

Yes, Arthur Needham's prattlings were certainly odd; it was intriguing to know that my father had once had a close friend who had ended up—to use his own word—a bugger, and my friends and I joked about it together: 'Do you suppose they went beddy-bye?'; but to give it serious consideration was another matter. An innocent explanation, after all, lay close at hand in my own young experience; the Count, like myself, may have started his emotional life (continuing it longer than I) by falling for young men whom he was unable to touch but worshipped from afar; his active and predatory homosexuality could have begun later. Indeed, so little thought, let alone suspicion, did I give to the relationship that I am vague now as to what I said to my father about the strange coincidence of my happening upon the Count's tracks. It would not have been easy to say much in any case to this old man with whom I had never had an intimate conversation and who never appeared to invite one, nor for that matter had I much to say, knowing little more about the Count than that he had started as a friend of my father's and ended as a friend of Arthur Needham's; to make insinuations about the latter association would have been out of the question, as also to appear suddenly and unprecedentedly interested in my father's past life. My recollection is that I mentioned, merely as an oddity, that my present landlord had known the Count de Gallatin who had lived and died round the corner from us in St Peter's Square in 1915, and that no particular interest was evinced in this item of news. I remember asking what the Count had been like, and my father, picking his nose, replied, 'A funny chap, a decent sort of fellow, most unfortunately jealous.' I believe I had the New Brighton photo with me—I had taken it to show to Arthur Needham—and asked what had happened to the fourth member of the group, Dudley Sykes. 'He married and died,' said my father briefly, returning to his newspaper.

Not long afterwards he himself fell ill and died, and the revelations of his secret orchard came out, to be followed, a couple of years later, by the information contained in the first sentence of this memoir. Under these successive blows—the first was shattering enough—the established image of the paterfamilias, the respectable, dull, suburban householder, the good, the poor, old dad, lay in pieces and needed reconstruction, yet it was not until about 1935 that I began to think seriously enough about him and myself to think us out on paper. Up till then he remained a curious and amusing subject for discussion among friends. I had indeed much else on my hands and mind, besides my sexual affairs, though I attach small importance to them now as excuses for inattention. Despairing of being a writer I took in 1928, as I have said, a job in the BBC; following my father's death I had the clearing up of his estate and the removal of my mother to the smaller house. Nevertheless, it seems that at this time a little more sunshine entered my life, fleetingly I fear, for I find among my papers a letter to me, dated July 16, 1930, which interests me as providing a portrait of myself in the late 'twenties. It is from that intellectual policeman I have mentioned, the friend to whom I owed so much, but whose character was so unstable and touchy, his demands upon friendship so impatient, that a mutual friend once said of him that he could not wait for the plants in his garden to grow but must be forever pulling them up to inspect their roots. The letter is written in anger, but anger is as valuable as alcohol for the communication of home truths. I forget the actual event that triggered this letter off, but I know that, like the barking dogs, he often got on my nerves with his constant unannounced invasion of my privacy and his inability to hold his indiscreet tongue in front of my sacred sailor, whom he himself had brought into my life. I suppose I must have had a conscience over my behaviour to him and sent him some tactless apology; the following, which did not sever our friendship, was his reply:

'For years now you've been sponging on your friends' energy by sitting gloomily about and letting them move around making excuses for you. I seem to have spent all my London life saying to myself "Poor old Joe" over something or other, but now that your excuses for gloom seem to be vanishing into thin air I am not going to let you pick on me. You must find something else to get a "vague uneasiness" over. I don't like you now and I am not going to let you worry me any longer.

I have had as much cause as you to be miserable. I've been lonely just as much as you; one hundred North

Country policemen are not company. You could have talked to me and wouldn't.

Since you've sneered all the affection out of me I find myself calmly thinking of you as "a miserable bloody tyke", and I can go to bed at night and get up in the morning several times and still think the same, which I've discovered as a fairly good test of whether I really believe a thing or am only pretending to myself.'

The 'excuses for gloom' which were 'vanishing into thin air' were, no doubt, the belated departure of my sister to Panama to attempt to restore her marital life, and the satisfactory settlement of my mother's financial future. In the same year Miss Louie died, Miss Emily came to take her place and I met her. Those readers who may be thinking I have held this card up my sleeve for new and startling disclosures will be disappointed. A dull, dutiful woman, she had nothing to say to my questions about my father, questions which could not have been particular since I did not then know what to ask. Yes, she remembered him and as a very handsome young man, what great friends he and the Count had been, and what a pity it had all come to such a sad end, she couldn't say why. I tried again later to speak to her, with no better result; as Arthur himself remarked when I mentioned my failure, 'Oh she was never a one to *talk*. Good gracious no! One can never get a *word* out of her, certainly not *against* anyone. Such a good, kind soul!'

Not long after this, when I was at the peak of my ability to be a 'miserable bloody tyke' owing to the rupture with my sailor, in the disconsolation of which I wallowed for a couple of years, Cis was discovered to have cancer which

sent him in and out of hospital, killing him at last; and
finding myself an inconvenience to Arthur, who talked of
selling the house, I moved into a smaller lodging nearby;
then, in 1934, to a flat in Maida Vale. It was here that, for
want of something to occupy such leisure time as was not
spent at the BBC or prowling the streets, I began to brood
over this story of my father and myself. It germinated, as I
have said, out of a sense of failure, of personal inadequacy,
of waste and loss; I saw it as a *stupid* story, shamefully stupid
that two intelligent people, even though parent and son
between whom special difficulties of communication are
said to lie, should have gone along together, perfectly
friendly, for so many years, without ever reaching the
closeness of an intimate conversation, almost totally igno-
rant of each other's hearts and minds. That I had also been
handed ready-made an unusual and startling tale did not
escape my journalist's eye. My father was a mystery man.
Part of his mystery had now been revealed; what about that
part of the picture which still lay in darkness, his early life
and relationship, so odd in view of Arthur Needham's
tittle-tattle, with the Count de Gallatin—and, for that
matter, with Mr Ashmore, these two wealthy gentlemen
in their thirties and the impecunious and uneducated young
guardsman in his 'teens, to whom they had both taken so
inordinate a fancy? Was not a man who was capable of so
much, capable of almost anything? Who could shed light
upon all this? It was very old history, but there were two
people still alive who might help, Arthur Stockley and
Uncle Denton, my father's younger brother, who lived in
South Africa. I started a correspondence with them both,
and the general information they sent me, such as it is, is

incorporated in the opening chapters of this memoir. From Stockley came the accounts of New Brighton and The Cell Farm, and that long impassioned private letter from Mme de Gallatin which I have quoted in full. And from him and Denton came the photographs of my father as a young man. These made me sit up. The inherent absurdity of envisaging my father in the arms of another man had never really faded; it faded now. It is true that, studying the photograph of him in uniform, I decided that I would not have picked him up myself; but the picture was said not to do him justice, and the better one Uncle Denton claimed to have he never managed to find. But from the photo of him as a young man-about-town it was not difficult to see why Ashmore and de Gallatin had fallen for him. Where and how had he met these two men? That was the crucial question. I put it to both my correspondents. Neither of them knew, or, if they knew they were not disposed to say. Nor did I feel, from my knowledge of them and the tone of their letters as my enquiries grew warmer, that insinuations or blunt questions would have any other effect than to bring the correspondence to an abrupt end: Denton indeed remarked in one letter, 'I enclose an answer to your family questions and will be pleased to answer any others *within reason.*' How vexing it was! What fun it would be if I could add the charge of homosexuality to my father's other sexual vagaries! What irony if it could be proved that he had led in his youth the very kind of life that I was leading! Where *had* these two men met him? Had they picked him up, as I picked guardsmen up, in the Napoleon or the Monkey Walk? Or was he 'ordered' through Mrs Truman before her shop was closed? For a friend of mine, who had a small library of erotica, had drawn my attention to a book which confirmed my belief that the behaviour of the guards of which I had learnt so much in my own time had been no different in my father's. This two-volume work was entitled *The Sins of the Cities of the Plain, or the Recollections of a Mary-Ann, with Short Essays on Sodomy and Tribadism*, and the relevant essay was called 'I Joined the Army', by Frank Griffin:

'Mr Fred Jones had been a soldier in the Foot Guards and brought out by Mr Inslip. It's the commonest thing possible in the Army. As soon as (or before) I had learned the goose-step, I had learned to be goosed. . . .

You can easily imagine that it is not so agreeable to spend half-an-hour with a housemaid when one has been caressed all night by a nobleman. This is the experience of all the men of my regiment, and I know it is the same in the First, the Blues, and every regiment of the Foot Guards. When a young fellow joins, some one of us breaks him in and teaches him the trick; but there is very little need of that, for it seems to come naturally to almost every young man. . . . We then have no difficulty in passing him on to some gentleman, who always pays us liberally for getting a fresh young thing for him.

Although of course we all do it for money, we also do it because we really like it, and if gentlemen gave us no money, I think we should do it all the same. So far as I can see, all the best gentlemen in London like running after soldiers, and I have letters from some of the very highest in the land. . . . There are lots of houses in London for it—I will give you a list some day—where only soldiers are received and where gentlemen sleep with them. The best known is now closed. It was the tobacconist's shop next door to Albany Street Barracks, Regent's Park, and was kept by a Mrs Truman. The old lady would receive orders from gentlemen and then let us know. . . . !'

This book was privately printed in 1881, two years after my father enlisted in the Blues at Albany Street Barracks.

Engaging speculations! Hoping still to drag him captive into the homosexual fold, I pursued my historical researches. Little could be expected from the Records Offices of the Blues and the Horse Guards, but I tried both and received copies of his certificates of discharge: conduct, alas, 'very good'. An attempt to dig deeper into the records of the Blues met with no success; the relevant ones, I was told, had unfortunately been destroyed in a fire. Searching through the back files of *The Times* I found the report of the lawsuit between my father and de Gallatin. This rather dejected me: if their relationship had been anything but above board, would my father have taken the risk of putting the 'vindictive' Count in the witness box in a dispute over money? Somerset House yielded me various death certificates and wills, including Ashmore's, and this reminded me of what seemed my last hope, Ashmore's son. Of this man I had private information, supplied by a close homosexual friend of mine and one-time colleague of his, that Air-Commodore Charlton I have already mentioned, that he too had indulged in homosexual practices, but furtively, screening himself by marriage and by denouncing and punishing the same practice in the ranks of his command. Whether

General Ashmore, a cold and wary figure, knew more about his father and mine than he disclosed in his interview with me I shall never know; all that I got out of him has already been related.

Baffled in all my enquiries I bethought me again of old Arthur Needham, with whom I had long been out of touch. Had I pumped him sufficiently? Had he, after all, the clue I so badly needed? Was he, for that matter, still alive? One weekend, in February, 1938, I went down to Hammersmith in search of him. No. 6 had been sold, but Arthur was living, I gathered, in a smaller house near the bridge. There I found him, with another dog, a tomcat thirteen years old and of enormous girth, and a housekeeper named Annie, to whom the cat belonged. He was lying cast down on his bed, sideways, as though he had fallen on it. I thought him ill or even dead, but he soon sat up and was between the two, a pitiable wreck, much thinner than I remembered him, gasping for breath. He was fully dressed—perhaps I had written and he was expecting me—but his housekeeper told me that he had not left the small house at all for eighteen months. Like some frightened animal with its back to the wall he was hiding from the death that had lately claimed Cis and Miss Emily. It was clearly useless to ask too much of him. From my notebook:

'I can't get me breath. Isn't it awful to be old? First it was Louie, then Cis, then Miss Emily, and I shall be the next.'

'Arthur dear, do tell me. Did your friend the Count de Gallatin ever say anything about having made love to my father?'

'Oh, the things you say! I'm as nervous as a kitten, the least thing sets me off. I can't even write a cheque now, me hand shakes so.'

'Arthur, it's important. Do you know about my father and the Count?'

'Oh, you couldn't ask the Count. But I had my ideas all the same.'

'I don't want ideas. I want facts. Did they go to bed together? *That* is what I want to know. Did the Count ever tell you anything?'

'Oh lord, you'll be the death of me! I think he did once say he'd had some sport with him. But me memory's like a saucer with the bottom out.'

I never saw old Arthur again, nor can I attach the least importance to 'some sport'. I expect he was trying to please me—and be rid of me. He died, aged seventy-eight, at the beginning of 1941. Before that, in 1940, a bomb fell outside my flat in Clifton Gardens, bringing the ceilings down. This put an end to my tenancy and to such fitful interest and sporadic attention as this memoir had been receiving. I did not look at it again for twenty years.

Eighteen

AFTER my father's death I moved my mother out of Blenheim House on Richmond Hill, the last of our three family residences. It was taken by Dr Wadd who had coveted it for some time as an annexe to his hydro next door (both houses and himself have long since been demolished). He offered to buy such fittings and furnishings as my mother would not need in the small box of a house we had found for her in Sheen Road. She selected what she wanted, the things she specially liked; the rest of the contents of the house, valuable curtains and carpets, silver, mountains of Blue Onion china, were sold to Wadd for a song. I remember a fine roomy Chesterfield in the drawing-room going for twelve and sixpence. This old friend of the family had always had an eye for the main chance. Owing to my work in the BBC I could take little part in these transactions, except to curb my mother's careless generosity. Particularly precious to her were sundry trunks, suitcases, bags and several large cardboard boxes. All these and whatever else she needed were transported to 159a Sheen Road. Here she lived for eleven years, 1930–1941.

She asked me if I would live with her—just the question, no pressure. It saddened me to say no; I could not have endured it. Instead a woman companion-help, whom she liked, was found for her and she had her little dog. I went constantly to see her and she was visited also by Aunt Bunny and the 'Doc', Air-Commodore Charlton and other friends of mine who were fond of her. For over a year she seemed perfectly happy, a merry little squirrel in its cage; then my sister announced her return with her child from Panama; she had failed to patch things up with her husband and was now divorced. There was no ready place for them to live in and my mother decided to have them stay with her. I tried to dissuade her from a step which, it seemed certain, was unlikely to suit anybody; the house was too tiny for such an invasion, she and my sister had never got on together, and my mother, who had had nothing to do with children since we were born and not much then, was surely too old and fixed in her habits now to be able to endure for long the addition of a small boy to her household. But she had set her heart on it, she was sorry for my sister in her adversity, had forgotten all the dissensions of the past and doubtless also wished to play the part of grand-mother. The results were as unpleasant as I had foreseen; by the time when, some years later, other accommoda-tion had been found for my sister, my mother had taken to living almost entirely in her bedroom, into which she would allow no one else to go, even her servant, and had also taken secretly to the bottle. Then the 'Doc' died and Aunt Bunny, left destitute, went to live with her in Sheen Road.

By the side of the house was a pretty *cul-de-sac* named Peldon Avenue, where the little Sealyham bitch got her exercise. One night, in September, 1941, a land-mine fell into it, cracking the house from top to bottom. My aunt happened to be away at the time; my mother and her servant were sleeping on mattresses in the sitting-room on the ground floor. Windows and doors blew in, the ceiling fell on them as they lay. In a panic the servant rushed out into the street in search of help. Returning, she found my mother standing in the dark, shattered room in her night shift, her hair full of plaster. 'I think it very inconsiderate of you,' said my mother reproachfully, 'to go out before sweeping up all this glass. I might easily have cut my feet.' The concussion had ruptured a small blood-vessel in one of her eyes; otherwise she was uninjured. She was seventy years old.

My sister, who was then living in a large block of furnished flats near by, found one for her and Aunt Bunny in the same building. It was here that, my mother's faculties rapidly failing, she made friends with the fly. Her furniture had to be removed from the wrecked house; I had it stored in a depository that had been improvised in Richmond Town Hall—upon which, soon afterwards, an incendiary bomb fell, burning everything up. Among the things that confronted my sister and me for disposal in my mother's sacred and filthy bedroom, with the great piles of ancient newspapers she had hoarded and the empty whisky bottles, was her personal luggage, her trunks and suitcases and those large cardboard boxes she had so carefully preserved. It was necessary to find out what they contained before deciding whether to store them or to take them along to her new flat—though, her memory going, if not gone, she asked for nothing and seemed hardly aware of what was happening in the world outside. I was personally curious too; I might find some useful information, letters, etc., about her early life with my father. I opened the cardboard boxes first. They were full of wastepaper. The wastepaper consisted of old receipts and circulars, letters, envelopes, Christmas cards, bits of Christmas crackers, newspaper cuttings about dress-making or cooking recipes, household lists and memoranda, old theatre programmes, visiting cards, blank pieces of paper, and literary compositions of her own—rambling verses and *pensées* in her large quill-pen writing; all these had been torn up into small fragments and put back into the boxes, which had then been secured with string. I opened her three square leather hat-boxes. They were full of wastepaper. There were two large cabin trunks. They were crammed with wastepaper. The drawers of her dressing table also contained wastepaper, excepting for two or three bundles of letters, tied with ribbon, from Harold Armstrong, my brother and myself. In the midst of this sea of torn-up paper various other objects were discovered: a few old and ragged small articles of clothing, some aged feathers and other trimmings for hats, empty jewel-cases, empty boxes, empty tins, old cosmetic and powder con-tainers, buttons, hairpins, desiccated suppositories, decayed De Reszke and Melachrino cigarettes, old and used sanitary towels done up in tissue paper, stumps of pencils, orange-wood sticks, Red Lavender lozenges. An occasional gold or silver trinket, of no value, was found, an occasional un-destroyed treasury note (£3. 10s. 0d. in all). Suddenly, for a time excitingly, bundles would appear like presents in a bran pie, done up in tissue paper and tied with ribbon or string, or large plain envelopes, bulging and sealed. They all contained wastepaper, torn into small fragments. To this mass of rubbish clung my mother's odour of 'Jicky' and Red Lavender lozenge. The last thing to be opened was an ancient battered black bag such as doctors used to carry. It was locked. No key could be found, but the leather had rotted, the bag was easily torn open. The first thing that met my eye was a page of pencilled writing in my mother's hand: 'Private. Burn without reading.' At last! Beneath were sundry packages tied up in ribbon. They were full of wastepaper. There was nothing else in the bag.

This was my mother's comment on life. It might serve also as a comment on this family memoir, which belongs, I am inclined to think, to her luggage. A good many questions have been asked, few receive answers. Some facts have been established, much else may well be fiction, the rest is silence. Of my father, my mother, myself, I know in the end practically nothing. Nevertheless I preserve it, if only because it offers a friendly, unconditional response to my father's plea in his posthumous letter: 'I hope people will generally be kind to my memory.'

Appendix

WHEN I had completed this so-called memoir, which remembers so little, a friend of mine who read it for me said I had fallen into the error of self-indulgence. The material contained in the present Chapter 12 was then rather more extensive and was divided into two chapters, for having started to examine my sexual psychology, so far as I was able, I became so interested in it that I worked it out to the end. My friend criticised this and I agreed with him; the book is *not* an autobiography, its intention is narrower and is stated in the title and the text, it is no more than an investigation of the relationship between my father and myself and should be confined as strictly as possible to that theme. I therefore removed two extraneous passages from my then Chapters 12 and 13, and telescoped those chapters into one. The book then came closer to its purpose and moved more swiftly in its pursuit of my lost and unknown father. But what was I to do with the excisions? The book had been a considerable sweat to write and they merited, I thought, a better fate than the wastepaper basket. Besides, I wanted to keep my dedication, which seems to me apt and just, and needed to state the reasons for it. For the interest therefore of psychologists in particular I have preserved these discarded pages in this appendix.

Another fact about my baffled sex life was that I was sexually incontinent, and of that I was deeply ashamed. I did not know then, as I have been told since, that it is a quite common affliction (although I must add that, to my annoyance, I have never been to bed with anyone who shared it) caused by anxiety, which I take to be a part of guilt, and might have been corrected by psychoanalysis. It was a great nuisance to me in many ways, and had a bad effect upon my conduct, if not upon my character. Whenever I was emotionally aroused, whenever I was in the presence of someone physically attractive whom I was wanting to embrace, or even when I was awaiting his arrival, I lived in a state of hot sexual excitement, the bulge of which in my trousers I was always afraid would be noticed. A kiss then, the mere pressure of an embrace, if I got as far as that, was enough to finish me off—and provide a new shame, that the stain, seeping through my trousers, might be seen. It may well have been this that, in my schooldays, sitting beside Jude in class and letting him guide my hand through the opened seam of his trouser pocket, precluded me, in my recollection, from requiring or desiring reciprocal treatment. I took to wearing tight jockey shorts to prop up against my stomach my betraying display, and later preferred double-breasted to open jackets as a further disguise.

This incontinence (to run ahead) had other deplorable results. It put an end to my own pleasure before it had begun and, with the expiry of my desire, which was never soon renewed, my interest in the situation, even in the person, causing me to behave inconsiderately to him; I have not been above putting an abrupt end to affairs with new and not highly attractive boys in whose first close embrace, and before taking off our clothes, I had already had my own complete, undisclosed satisfaction. Apart from the probability that I did not then want to go further, how could I go further and reveal to someone who had not yet reached a state of erection the mess I had made of myself? Even a little friendly moralising at such moments as a wriggle out: 'Perhaps we oughn't to be doing this', has not been beyond my capabilities. It may well be that the final disappointing of that Cambridge boy who stayed in my Richmond home was due to this, that through a kiss and the mere thought of taking him to bed I had already had my orgasm.

If this life I am prowling about in were someone else's and I its historian (which in fact is the way I am trying to see it), I would rub my hands gleefully over some of the poems I wrote and published in Cambridge. What can these curious productions mean unless that although I regarded myself as free, proud and intellectually unassailable as a homosexual, I was profoundly riddled with guilt? Two in particular seem to me so shocking that I wonder how I ever came to publish them. One is called 'On a Photograph of Myself as a Boy'. Of its five over-loaded stanzas two will suffice:

My younger self, what were you musing on
So gladly in that calm, sequestered place?
Your young beliefs are now forever gone,
And gone the peace that lighted then your face.
What was the dream of love in which you shone
　　With such enchanted grace?...

[211]

Let me go back! Let me go back to you!
And we will learn some pleasant games to play,
And choose some other fancy to pursue. . . .
Oh why did you not put your dream away,
Unhappy boy, when it was faint and new
    And held you not in sway?

The other poem is similar and even worse. It also is about
a picture—'The Portrait of a Mother'. Five stanzas may be
too many to stomach, but I will quote five:

Your calm eyes watch me as I pace the floor;
Across the room and back they follow me:
Calm eyes, calm eyes, what do you watch me for,
    Calm eyes that cannot see?. . . .

Oh watch me not! In quest of solitude
I turn among the shadows as I pace;
But I have not the power to elude
    The vigil of your face. . . .

What do you see? That fixed relentless look
Searching my visage seems to learn from it.
The face of man is not an open book
    In which his sins are writ. . . .

You look and shrink . . . as though I had betrayed
Some sacred trust laid on me by a child;
Or smothered Love in secret as he played,
    Smothered him as he smiled.

Why do you move beside me as I move?
Oh close your eyes and shut my thoughts from me!
It was too beautiful . . . the face of Love . . .
    For my mortality.

What my poor mother, the last person in the world to
wear a 'fixed relentless look', thought of this poem I don't
remember; I suppose she must have read it. It is interesting
to observe that it is, in different form, the same poem as
'Millstones', the one I published in my school magazine
The Wasp some seven or eight years earlier. Although I
wrote the two poems just quoted at Cambridge, I cannot
now recall whether I was still chaste, in the sense of not
having been to bed with anyone.

How much of all this did I enjoy, this long pursuit of love
through sex, out of which, in the end, I emerged as lonely
as I began? The moods of the past are difficult to recapture.
The orgasm itself is a pleasure of course—had I not always
placed it first among the pleasures?—but its pleasure has
degrees. When things suited me and I felt relaxed I enjoyed
it. But I was seldom quite suited or relaxed. If my prejudices were gradually ditched, my anxieties remained; experience, from which we are said to learn, has no effect upon
the inner nature. A new form of anxiety, a maddening impotence, began to afflict me. I can put no date to it, it emerged in the company of my old stand-bys, my few steadies. I
believe it had nothing to do with increasing age, nothing
to do with sexual exhaustion; although so many boys had
passed through my hands I lived with none of them, they
came and went, sometimes to return, at no point in this

journey did I have a feeling of stability, of more than momentary satisfaction. Indeed when, some time in the 'thirties, a friend asked me if I had any notion how many boys
I'd taken to bed, I was astonished to find that those I managed to recollect got into three figures, for I never had any
sense of riches, only of poverty, and at last of dire poverty.
The impotence that started to defeat me was neurotic. I was
still close to incontinence with new experiences—becoming
rarer and rarer—with that deserter, for instance, that last,
long emotional affair, who had not yet flashed upon my
sexual scene; with old friends things began to go 'wrong',
and with him also when he became an old friend. I
looked forward eagerly in my poverty to seeing them
when they could get away from their various units, to
having their hands upon me and the use of their bodies;
they knew what I wanted though they seldom wanted it
themselves, and this hitherto I had not minded so long as I
got my own comfortable satisfaction. Now I began to mind.
Like the irksome, unsmotherable pea beneath the prin-
cess's mattresses, some fret would enter my head. In spite of
my theories about sex, I had always found it hard to impose
my wishes (further evidence of guilt no doubt), to go
straight for the thing I most desired, and since these boys
were normal they either had no such wishes to impose or
left it all to me. The Welsh boy alone sometimes took the
initiative, though, being newly married, he wanted
nothing for himself. Excepting for him, and throughout my
life now that I come to think of it, no one whom I wanted,
from my sailor onwards, even when mutual desires were
involved, ever took the physical initiative; it was always
left to me who found it difficult to take, and this, no doubt,

was a situation I myself had created—and because of its frustration, perhaps desired. I seemed always to be pretending not to have an erection, not to be impatient and that the quid that usually passed between us at once (the boys were always short of cash) was not a *quid pro quo* but a gift. Now it began to defeat me, this situation with old friends who did not desire me and whom I myself no longer desired so much as the thing they had to give, if only I could get it. The fret would enter. . . . Why had I taken him to the pub first? it was getting late, I must hurry. . . . Why had I not taken him to the pub first? he was bored, I must hurry. . . . Why had I let him have his own satisfaction first? he was tired, I must hurry. . . . I was taking too long, he was only being obliging and my sweat and the weight of my body must be disagreeeable to him, I must hurry, hurry. . . . Then the slow collapse, and nothing that he could do, or I could do in the way of furious masturbation, could retrieve the wretched failure.

In the mid- 'thirties I began to keep a day-to-day diary. I had developed another of my theories—self-defensive it now looks—that there was not the slightest need to seek material for travel books, as writers usually did, by going off to foreign parts, climbing mountains, living with primitive tribes, pioneering down untrodden paths if any were left; everyone's life, said I, even the veriest bank clerk's in Manchester or Little Pidlington, was crammed with the most exciting interest and adventure if only he would observe and describe it. Let anyone keep a candid, detailed diary for a year, noting down *everything* that happened to him day by day, in his life, in his mind, and a book would emerge far more fascinating, however clumsily written, than if he had been anthropologising among the Pygmies or sliding about on Arctic ice. My own diary lasted some six months, hastily scrawled because my nocturnal ramblings, all described, took up so much of my time. Then I got bored and discontinued it. Fifteen years later I came upon it again, read it through and instantly destroyed it, as though it were an evil thing. The evil was in the misery. It contained no single gleam of pleasure or happiness, no philosophy, not even a joke; it was a story of unrelieved gloom and despondency, of deadly monotony, of frustration, loneliness, self-pity, of boring 'finds', of wonderful chances muffed through fear, of the latchkey turned night after night into the cold, dark, empty flat, of railings against fate for the emptiness and wretchedness of my life. It also contained, the saddest thing of all, my critical comments upon my first meeting with that Welsh boy, now dead, his dullness and smelly feet.

At the time when I read this diary I was happy at last. It is, for me, the interesting part of this personal history that peace and contentment reached me in the shape of an animal, an Alsatian bitch. Is it, I wonder, of any value as a clue to my psychology to recall that in my play *The Prisoners of War* the hero, Captain Conrad (myself of course), unable to build on human relations, takes to a plant? He tells some story of another imprisoned officer who fell in love with a pet rabbit and read short stories to it out of a magazine. 'Plants or rabbits,' he says, 'it's the same thing.' This bitch of mine entered my life in the middle 'forties and entirely transformed it. I have already described her in two books; it is necessary to say here that I don't believe there was anything special about her, except that

[216]

she was rather a beauty. In this context it is not she herself but her effect upon me that I find interesting. She offered me what I had never found in my sexual life, constant, single-hearted, incorruptible, uncritical devotion, which it is in the nature of dogs to offer. She placed herself entirely under my control. From the moment she established herself in my heart and home, my obsession with sex fell wholly away from me. The pubs I had spent so much of my time in were never revisited, my single desire was to get back to her, to her waiting love and unstaling welcome. So urgent was my longing every day to rejoin her that I would often take taxis part-way, even the whole way, home to Putney from my London office, rather than endure the dawdling of buses and the rush-hour traffic jams in Park Lane. I sang with joy at the thought of seeing her. I never prowled the London streets again, nor had the slightest inclination to do so. On the contrary, whenever I thought of it, I was positively thankful to be rid of it all, the anxieties, the frustrations, the wastage of time and spirit. It was as though I had never wanted sex at all, and that this extraordinary long journey of mine which had seemed a pursuit of it had really been an attempt to escape from it. I was just under fifty when this animal came into my hands, and the fifteen years she lived with me were the happiest of my life.

One of my friends, puzzled by the sudden change in my ways, asked me whether I had sexual intercourse with her. It may be counted as something on the profit side of my life that I could now receive such a question intelligently. I said no. In truth, her love and beauty when I kissed her, as I often did, sometimes stirred me physically; but although I had to cope with her own sexual life and the frustrations

I imposed upon it for some years, the thought of attempting to console her myself, even with my finger, never seriously entered my head. What little I did for her in her burning heats—slightly more than I admitted in *My Dog Tulip*—worried me in my ignorance of animal psychology, in case, by gratifying her clear desires, which were all addressed to me, I might excite and upset her more than she was already excited and upset. The most I ever did for her was to press my hand against the hot swollen vulva she was always pushing at me at these times, taking her liquids upon my palm. This small easement was, of course, nearer the thing she wanted than to have her back, tail and nipples stroked. Yet looking at her sometimes I used to think that the Ideal Friend, whom I no longer wanted, perhaps never had wanted, should have been an animal-man, the mind of my bitch, for instance, in the body of my sailor, the perfect human male body always at one's service through the devotion of a faithful and uncritical beast.

I must not, however, give the impression that I went entirely without sex during my years with this animal. I no longer ran after it or even thought of it in England, but at least twice here it offered itself to me, unsought and unexpected, and whenever I went abroad I found myself pursuing it again. I did not go abroad much, I preferred to spend my holidays with my bitch, but on the few occasions that I left her, when she was getting old and inactive, and went to France, Italy, Greece and Japan, I looked for sexual adventure and found it. Into it were once more imported all the old anxieties and worries, heartbreaks even, that had attended it throughout my life—with the latest anxiety, to which I have alluded, added: impotence. This anxiety, to which perhaps all my other anxieties had been tending and was their last phase, now took charge. I never approached any bed without the worry: 'Shall I be able to function?' I would try, sometimes in advance of a meeting, sometimes with closed eyes during the desirable but fearful act, to put myself into a prosperous frame of mind, telling myself that I was perfectly unworried, comfortable, welcome, free, safe and happy, that everything was exactly 'right'. Sometimes I managed; often the very fear perhaps of the frustration and humiliation of failure caused me to fail.

About the Author

J. R. Ackerley (1897–1976) was the literary editor of *The Listener*, the B.B.C. magazine, from 1935 until 1959. He was a brilliant editor, tireless traveler, and a prolific correspondent. His other books include *My Dog Tulip*, *Hindoo Holiday*, and *We Think the World of You*. He lived most of his life in London.